OUR FRAGMENTED WORLD

OUR
FRAGMENTED
WORLD

Ronald Harvey

GREEN BOOKS

First published in 1988 by
Green Books
Ford House, Hartland
Bideford, Devon EX39 6EE

© Ronald Harvey 1988

Typeset by Computype, Exeter

Printed by Hartnoll
Victoria Square, Bodmin, Cornwall

British Library Cataloguing in Publication Data

Harvey, Ronald
Our fragmented world.
1. Western world. Society
I. Title
909'.098210–828

ISBN 1–87009810–2

I would like to record my indebtedness, first of all to my wife Audrey who made the original suggestion for this book, secondly to Satish Kumar without whose help and encouragement it would not have been published, and finally to Rodney Aitchtey for his advice and work on preparation of the manuscript.

The world does not hold thee; thou thyself art the world which so strongly imprisons thee.

(Angelus Silesius 1624–77)

Firstly there is the unity in things whereby each thing is at one with itself, consists of itself and coheres to itself. Secondly there is the unity whereby one creature is united with the others and all parts of the world constitute one world.

(Pico della Mirandola 1463–94)

Man, for example, is related to all that he knows. He needs a place to hold him, time to exist in, motion in which to live, elements to form him, warmth and food to nourish him, air to breathe. He sees light, he feels bodies; in short he has a relationship with everything . . . . Since everything, therefore, is both cause and effect, dependent and supporting, mediate and immediate, and everything is held together by a natural and imperceptible chain which binds the most distant and the most different things together, I consider it impossible to know the parts without the whole, and impossible to know the whole without knowing each part separately.

(Blaise Pascal 1623–62)

How dreadful is this place! This is none other than the House of God and the Gate of Heaven.

(Thomas Traherne 1637–74)

Contents

Foreword

'In the beginning of things Chaos was created', said Hesiod. It could be applied to Ronald Harvey's collection of *aperçus* and reflections which began as unconnected notes.

This stimulating book gives an encyclopaedic view of our world which appears to be on the verge of destroying itself. It explains why this is so, and offers balanced suggestions about how the dangerous trends can be contained. *Our Fragmented World* has the distinction of not encouraging despair because its author believes that it is enough to change direction in one's daily life. The effort of making the change is worthwhile in itself. If enough people did change direction, the future would be changed also.

The contents were not written in a consecutive order, and therefore it's not necessary to read them in the order you find them. Open the book at random and benefit from the conclusions of a lifetime's concern.

Rodney Aitchtey
Peckham Rye, March 1988

The words on the shining brass plate have become indistinguishable.

The front door opens.

A figure with the face of a sage with thin white beard stands in the doorway.

'Please follow me'

gently up a staircase to a room at the top of the house where roofs and chimney pots are company; it is the consulting room.

Who is Ronald Harvey?

He has been practising osteopathy for the past thirty-five years; thirteen years in the East India Dock area of Limehouse, and at Toynbee Hall in Stepney. He was brought up into a strong conservative tradition which was reinforced by school; anything else that existed was political and undesirable. After school, which he disliked, he led a wide-ranging life. He canoed the length of France from north to south, and then cycled into Italy from Marseilles. He helped run a farm in Colonial Africa, and prospected for gold. He ended up in Paris, shortly before the Second World War, in the flat where Mahatma Gandhi had stayed, and did his small part in disseminating Gandhi's philosophy. The war came and he was swept up into serving to destroy Nazism; he came to play a curious role in undercover intelligence. After the war, he joined his wife in André Deutsch's first publishing venture. After two years there he became a scriptwriter and producer of Schools Broadcasts at the BBC. Then he qualified to be an osteopath after four years training. When CND was formed, he and his wife joined.

Who is his wife?

Audrey Harvey was a regular contributor on housing matters over the years to the *New Statesman*. She wrote the influential pamphlet, *Casualties of the Welfare State,* out of which arose the television film on homelessness, *Cathy Come Home*. Shelter recently published her, *In court for the rates . . . and the poll tax* and *How to become a lay advocate*. Both the Citizens' Rights Office and the Lay Advocacy Service for the Law Courts owe their existence to her initiative.

Well, well. If we accept that the ideal couple is one where each influences the other equally in multiple ways, an unexpected flowering can occur. Ronald Harvey at 77 years old is now the diffident author of *Our Fragmented World,* as well as being the osteopath practising at the Nature Cure Clinic in London. Its patron, until his death earlier this year (April 1988) at the age of ninety-nine, was Lord Fenner Brockway. Doesn't it suggest there may be something in whole living for longevity?

R.A.

Preface

Our Fragmented World is the result of trying to accommodate myself to living in a world apparently committed to sophisticated methods of self-advancement for the few, deprivation for the many, the increasingly rapid exhaustion of the earth's resources, and the threat of nuclear destruction for all.

It consists of a number of thoughts and conclusions thrown up during a chequered career in an attempt to make some sense of the situation in which our leaders have chosen to place us, and to which we have all, wittingly or unwittingly, contributed.

Many of these thoughts are of a political nature, but I am not naturally a political animal. I belong to no political party and indeed find difficulty in supporting any party, and always have. I vote, without enthusiasm, for what I consider the less dangerous, or the less restrictive, or the more equitable of the choices on offer. It is, in effect, a negative vote, for to my mind politicians of whatever colour have not yet woken up to the sort of world we are living in. They may know about the past and be careful about looking after their own back-yard and solicitous for those who support them, but they seem to have a myopic view of the future, are careless of the third world and largely regardless of the effect of their policies on the wider world and posterity in general. Perhaps one is asking too much of politicians, but perhaps also one should ask a little more.

Much of the trouble appears to be that the tone of the world has been increasingly set by the technological superiority of the west and its emphasis on growth. 'Get rich quick while one can' is, no doubt, a plausible philosophy for the greedy, but not for those exploited in the process, nor is it of much comfort to posterity, for at the rate the exploitation is expanding there will soon be little of the earth's riches left to plunder, let alone share out, for fair shares has rarely been much more than an idealistic pipe-dream.

Nevertheless the signs are that a change may be on the way. Even those obsessed with growth are beginning to realize that there are limits, even to growth. In recent years never has so much been written in favour of a change of course, of a reassessment of man's place in nature, of a recognition that we and our world are one, and that we can't continue to go on cutting off our nose because we are greedy for the taste of it.

This book was originally written as a series of disjointed notes on various subjects and now has been brought together. It tried to show how the world appeared to me – a confusing array of conflicting, often mutually annihilating interests. But appearances are not everything and I have tried to look beyond them, convinced that at bottom there is unity, order and harmony yet to be found.

My opinions have changed with experience. It is often said that if one is a radical in youth one becomes a conservative in later life. Indeed there is nothing like the acquisition of wealth or the onset of middle age for turning a revolutionary red into a self-satisfied blue. Experience has taught me otherwise. Neither the red nor the blue attract me. My orientation is at right-angles to both opposite poles; it is towards the 'Greens'.

Introduction

Without belief in the inner harmony of our world there would be no
science.

Einstein

All entities or factors in the universe are essentially relevant to each other's
existence.

A.N. Whitehead

This book is entitled *Our Fragmented World*. It is fragmented because we
have fragmented it. Yet, essentially, it is 'all of a piece'. The whole is not a
meaningless mass. Meaning lurks in every cranny, shines in every shaft of
sunlight. Form and structure may quarter the world for us but they also, at
the same time, unite it. The geographical and cosmographical co-
ordinates by which we orientate ourselves in space can be seen reflected in
our buildings, our cities, our laws and our religions as well as in our
science. Even the way we speak, our choice of words, our alphabet, our
language conform to structures which run deep in earth and psyche. Such
structures are communicating links, connecting threads which we have
too often regarded as barriers.

The meaning of the ancient four elements did not, as Plato
emphasized, stop at actual Fire, Air, Earth and Water. It reached not only
deep into the quality of matter but also into mind, presenting us with a
meaningful framework for the association of ideas, as well as a guide to
the psyche itself. Structure and function run through everything. Pattern
is everywhere, interlinking patterns, criss-crossing patterns, patterns in
time as well as in space. Rhythm is everywhere and everywhen, in 'the
dance of Shiva', in the revolution of the solar system, in the seasons, in the
rising and setting of sun and moon, in the blood, in the cells, in our daily
'circadian' pulsations. Number and proportion reveal themselves in
plants, in animals, as well as in cathedrals and temples. We find such
structures because we are thus programmed. They are there and at the
same time we put them there. Our world and ourselves are one. Subject
and object are found to be the same. We are what we experience.

We and our world form part of an organic whole. We are sewn into the

1

fabric. The old idea that man is a microcosmic reflection of the macrocosm is not far short of the truth. When we despoil nature for our own advantage we may be better off materially for the time being but are worse off in any other sense. When we pollute and rape nature we do it to ourselves. Eastern philosophies have long recognized the one-ness of things, while western science has chosen to concentrate on difference, on splitting, fragmenting and specializing. Until recently western science has taken an attitude to knowledge reflecting that of certain politicians to people – the attitude of 'apartheid' (separate development) resulting in the method of 'reductionism'. The old Latin precept 'Divide et impera' (divide and rule) no doubt helped to keep Rome in power as today it keeps any autocracy in power, but it is a strategy for manipulation not for understanding. With science, too, manipulation has outstripped understanding. Now, however, with the advent of sub-atomic and particle physics scientists are being forced to reconsider their assumptions. Indeed we can no longer consider ourselves as mere observers. We are all participators. Whether we like it or not we are right in it, all the way.

Consider one link between micro- and macro-cosm. Take a whirlpool or vortex. The vortex rotates slowly on the outside, rapidly on the inside. This relates to the rotation of the solar system – the farther out you go the slower the revolution. The vortex in its movement mirrors the whole planetary system, so that we can regard the whole visible cosmos as a vast vortex. Now if one puts a small stick into the circle of a whirlpool it will always point in the original direction however fast or slowly it whirls round the circle. It is as if connected by microscopic filaments to the visible boundaries of our universe, the fixed stars.

From another point of view the unity and coherence of the cosmos can be brought to our attention by the hologram, a kind of three-dimensional image developed with a laser and producing a photographic transparency. In the hologram every part of the whole contains or implies the whole. If you take a hologram of a house and cut it in two you get not two halves but two whole houses. Each portion, however much you cut it, contains the entire image. The subject of a hologram cannot be divided into fragments for what should have been a fragment turns out to be a whole. From this point of view a fragmented world is impossible. Moreover, the hologram is not just a trick of vision or an exciting invention; it relates to the fundamental units of matter which, science now recognizes, cannot be split up as individual bits or building blocks. Indeed the holographic mode appears to govern the structure of life and the structure of consciousness and thinking processes as well. It suggests that if we are to live in this holographic world the best way of doing it would appear to be 'holistically'. We must learn to think and act in wholes.

However, the upshot of this would mean the breaking down of class barriers, race barriers, national barriers, the difference between rich and poor, privileged and under-privileged. It would outlaw racialism, nationalism, greed, envy, oppression and aggression. The end of divisiveness would imply the end of *laissez-faire* capitalism. If holism is to take over then such barriers must come down. If they do, the sort of society we have known collapses for it is such barriers that have maintained it.

'Man is born free; and everywhere he is in chains' wrote Jean Jacques Rousseau in the first line of his *Social Contract*. Sometimes the chains are political, sometimes economic, sometimes religious, conventional, traditional or habitual. A first move should be to strike off the fetters of established thinking for as we think so do we act, and it is thinking the way we do that has got us into the mess we are in. Let us take the idea of property. Personal property is considered a good thing to have, and the more the better. We in the West are urged to invest in property, to acquire it, to develop it, to maximize it. Those who have it are looked up to; those who haven't are looked down on. It would appear from this that the greatest amount of property held by the largest number of people would ensure happiness for all.

But Rousseau's *Social Contract* also says, 'The first man who, having enclosed a piece of ground, bethought himself of saying *This is mine,* and found people simple enough to believe him, was the real founder of civil society. From how many crimes, wars and murders, from how many horrors and misfortunes might not any one have saved mankind, by pulling up the stakes, or filling up the ditch, and crying to his fellows, "Beware of listening to this impostor; you are undone if you once forget that the fruits of the earth belong to us all, and the earth itself to nobody." ' From property 'there arose rivalry and competition on the one hand, and conflicting interests on the other, together with a secret desire on both of profiting at the expense of others. All these evils were the first effects of property, and the inseparable attendants of growing inequality.'

In this country and in some others, the common property is being increasingly sold up, parcelled out and handed over; not to those most in need of it but to those who have the money to buy it. Already those with few shares are being bought out by those with many shares while those with none, i.e. the vast majority, will, as always, have next to nothing. Since property feeds power and power underpins property we have increasingly a powerless majority at the mercy of a dominant minority.

If, with Rousseau, we regard the earth as the property of no man, no tribe, no nation, no firm, no trust, no international consortium, but as land in trust for all mankind certain things follow. The rape of the earth for the benefit of those who already have too much at the expense of those who have too little becomes unthinkable. The precious land would no longer be pillaged for cash crops for the over-rich and over-fed but farmed for subsistence crops to feed everyone. Oilfields would not be exhausted to supply the enormous energy requirements of technological growth in the western world. Nuclear energy would become superfluous except to keep western households in luxury. It would not be needed for the simple basic technology best suited to farming the planet for the benefit of all.

We can think with the logic of reason and we can feel the injustice of it all, but we perpetuate it with our actions. Greed and aggression are too strong for us. We put both down to natural instinct which absolves us from doing too much about it. It is, we believe, man's nature, a nature inherited from his animal ancestors. Man must eat and protect himself and his family. Acquisitiveness may be necessary up to a point, but it is not necessary to buy up thousands of acres of land, or take over tribal lands. The ability to protect oneself is again a necessity, but this need not involve murder of one's neighbour, violence against others, and least of all war against other members of the species.

Aggression and greed often go hand in hand. Sometimes the military follow the merchants, sometimes the merchants follow the military. Much of history has been built on the activities of this unpleasant pair. If aggression is the father of war, greed is the mother of wealth and poverty, boom and slump, glut and scarcity. They have a number of poor relations and a rabble of hangers-on: street violence, thuggery, theft, sharp practice, grievous bodily harm, and robbery with violence. Their richer relations have insider dealing, embezzlement, property scandals, take-over bids, the activities of the stock market, company frauds and the dubious machinations of huge international firms. The unfortunate children of such parents are over-consumption in the west and famine in the third world.

We have been able to shrug off responsibility for our aggression in the belief that it is a natural instinct inherited from our animal ancestry. However, despite popular belief we have no such inheritance. Human beings are much more aggressive than animals, aggressive at the drop of a hat, or even at the thought of a hat being dropped. Animals are aggressive only when they need to be. An ape will 'see off' another ape but not kill it. A troop of monkeys will never conspire together to destroy another such troop. The same cannot be said of man. If what has come down to us from our relatively peaceable primate ancestors cannot be held solely responsible for the violence and aggression exhibited by so-called civilized man one is obliged to cast a suspicious eye at the environment.

The influence of environment begins long before birth. It begins at the beginning, with our genes. Genes do not exist *in vacuo*. They are part of their environment as we are part of our world. They are, as it were, 'sewn into' their environment as we are to ours. No organism ever develops without an environment. It is not inheritance *per se* but the interaction between inheritance and environment where the responsibility must be placed.

Men are not innately violent or murderous; they learn to be so. Their text book for learning is the environment. One should, however, not limit the word environment to the surrounding physical milieu, because it includes the mental, emotional, tribal, national, religious or racial ambience in which people have been brought up and which they accept as normal. The environment embraces conventions, laws, traditions, customs, habits, and so on, for we shape our environment as it in turn shapes us. The word environment might perhaps be replaced by the word 'context', for context embraces meaning. Without context there is no meaning, no pattern, no form within which to operate. A context also supplies us with norms, limits, stimuli, obstructions and opportunities.

When an animal is taken out of its natural environment and placed in another its behaviour changes. Rats in overcrowded cages can become very aggressive. They are faced with obstructions and few opportunities and their natural energies are turned against each other. Something similar occurs with the human animal. Growing up without money in an inner city slum the human animal can become violent and anti-social. Mugging, vandalism, and inter-racial violence may, and often do, follow. Such behaviour is much more rare if the environment is a pleasant one, a leafy suburb or a country town with room to breathe. Inner city dwellers are not innately more violent; they become so through the pressures of their environment.

Violence feeds on violence and breeds violence. In a violent age violence on the streets is mirrored by violence in sport and violence on television. And since the continual depiction of violence on television tends to make people regard it as a normal concomitant of modern civilization, any natural revulsion to its use is correspondingly weakened. It is said in defence of violence on television that there is no proof that people are influenced by it, but advertisers know better. They are convinced of the effect of television and back their conviction to the tune of hundreds of thousands of pounds. Violence on television fosters violence in real life which in turn fosters further violence on television. Fact feeds fiction and fiction feeds fact. We have constructed a context in which violence is considered normal and self-perpetuating.

Greed, like aggression, is not an instinct either. Greed is the proliferation of acquisitiveness beyond the bounds of necessity, usually at the expense of others. Animals in their natural state are not greedy. When they are hungry they eat their fill, but no more. They do not pile up personal possessions. Enough is enough. With the human animal, on the other hand, enough is not nearly enough. 'Having' is all important, 'being' less so. We become little more than what we possess. We have become an appendage to greed. So to some extent has our whole way of life. We could not live the way we do without greed, for greed is at the base of the system. To say that greed is an instinct is an insult to our whole animal ancestry. We learn to be greedy. Moreover we are implored by every device of advertising to become yet more greedy. Greed is assiduously taught and eagerly absorbed.

If greed and aggression are acquired rather than being basic instincts, then our future may not look so bleak for it means we can do something about it. We do not have to have wars, nor do we have to live in a hyper-acquisitive consumer society. If it can change us, then we can change it.

A besetting error in man's view of his place in nature is to jettison involvement in favour of separation, to prefer division to unity, discord to harmony, individualism to altruism, the part to the whole. This has not always been so. Once man felt himself to be very much a part of nature. He felt it in his bones. He felt at one with the rivers, the trees, the mountains. He deified them as nymphs, dryads and oreads, or saw nature as the 'dance of Shiva'. Everything had meaning, everything connected with everything else, and humans were part of that meaning.

The Enlightenment changed everything, at least for western man. The Enlightenment was our Tree of Knowledge and we grabbed at its fruit. In spite of the warnings of poets like Blake and Wordsworth the serpent of knowledge bit deeply into our world. Unity and wholeness were out; division was in. The dualism of Descartes set the ball rolling and the science of the 'natural philosophers' was rapidly overtaken by the science of 'reductionism'. The all-round learning and competence of Renaissance man was replaced by specialization; branches of learning were sundered from other branches and treated as though there was no connection between them. True, the corpus of knowledge was growing so fast and so large that some specialization was inevitable, being beyond the competence of a single person to encompass. What was lacking was a science of integration which would link parts with whole with an appreciation of the necessity, and yet more, a desire to do so.

Recently, however, the appreciation and the desire have been revived in the growing concept of holism, by the 'Green' movement, by ecologists and conservationists everywhere. The science of integration may still be lacking but with a changing climate of opinion and a favourable wind it is not beyond the bounds of possibility for such a science to emerge naturally, organically.

A further consideration is that where generalization leads to flexibility, specialization leads to rigidity. Where flexibility fosters life, rigidity favours death. Specialism is hostile to life, to development, for it narrows and eventually closes all routes to change. The ant is an example of specialized perfection and after sixty million years it remains as it ever was. The dinosaur, too, as fine an example of specialism as one could find, was unable to adapt to a changing environment and became extinct.

A powerful adjunct to specialization is technology, the very proliferation of which not only destroys environment but puts machines before people. It comes between people and people, between management and worker. Employees are right to be worried. It facilitates the treatment of people as objects for manipulation. Technology cannot feel. It puts the control of the many in the hands of a few to an extent not hitherto possible. Technology on a large scale is no friend of democracy but a powerful ally of dictatorship. While such technology is a threat to any humane, caring society, the same is not true for all technology. Technology on a small scale, for the peasant, for the African village, for the Indian 'sudras' and 'untouchables', for the peons of Latin America, for small-holders in Europe, for small communities and co-operatives it can be a boon. But in the sort of society in which we live that sort of technology is of little concern. It is the big stuff that matters and, as ever, it is the big stuff that holds the little stuff down.

Our world is split again between the claims of individualism and altruism. The proper field of individualism is internal, within oneself, that of altruism external, between ourselves and others. We do not seem to have fully appreciated this and have let individualism loose in altruism's territory. There is a lot to be said for 'rugged individualism' as romantics like to call it, but rugged individualism at the expense of others has often led to riches amongst grinding poverty. The internal

7

individualist, the individualist in ideas is to be welcomed – the Galileos, the Newtons, the Einsteins – but the external individualist in pursuit of money and power regardless of the consequences to others is a menace to any decent society. The external individualist does not like public services for such a one does not need them, or not to the extent that others do. External individualists do not like state schools for they do not need them; they can pay for a 'private' school. They do not like public hospitals for they can pay for private hospital care. They do not like public transport; they have a car. The result we see all too often in our cities – private affluence for those at the top, public squalor for the rest.

Rugged individualism is too often a euphemism for ruthless selfishness. In the latest pages in the history of evolution it has succeeded in making egotists out of those biologically best fitted to function as altruists. Neo-Darwinists have helped to paint the picture by narrowing Darwin's theory to a ruthless struggle for existence, a nature 'red in tooth and claw'. But Darwin himself in *The Descent of Man* pointed out that in numerous animal groups the struggle for the means of existence was replaced by co-operation. The fittest were not necessarily the strongest, nor the cleverest. In Darwin's words, 'Those communities which included the greatest number of the most sympathetic members would flourish best and rear the greatest number of offspring.' This view has been confirmed over and over again by numerous observers. A century before, Rousseau, in his *Discourse on the Origin of Inequality,* wrote of compassion: 'that the very brutes themselves sometimes give evident proofs of it'. Kropotkin, too, in his *Mutual Aid* gives hundreds of instances of animals helping other animals and goes further, pursuing his thesis from animals to savages, to mutual aid in the medieval city, to mutual aid in modern times. In our own day the anthropologist Ashley Montagu brings further evidence in his *Darwin, Competition and Co-operation* and also in his *The Direction of Human Development.* If mutual aid is a fundamental factor in the survival of a species, then it would appear that to help others is also to help ourselves.

Unfortunately we still believe in the survival of the most ruthless. We still believe also in a mechanistic nineteenth-centuryish world, one that we are separate from and can manipulate for our own advantage, and that we can get away with these things without getting caught up by the consequences. We believe it because we are taught it. But we are like flies in a spider's web. Each step we take enmeshes us still further, and with us everyone else.

Nature, however, is not so passive a victim as one might think. Even her exhaustion on our behalf is beginning to rebound on us. Moreover a certain cunning appears to be creeping into nature's defence tactics. Some years ago we thought to bring about a mass destruction of rabbits – myxomatosis. What happened? Nature, upset that her balance was being disturbed so suddenly and ruthlessly, fought back and it was not long before rabbits immune to myxomatosis began to be born.

Then antibiotics were invented, to supplement the body's auto-immune system where it seemed inadequate. But soon antibiotics, a great source of profit for international pharmaceutical companies, were being prescribed for trivialities of all kinds. When it was found that they had side-effects, some of them serious, so great is the pressure of profit, they continued to be fed, together with hormones, to chickens, cattle, pigs, and who knows what else, for human consumption. Many such tamperings with nature are now known to be cancer forming. The next step, presumably, is to pile anti-carcinogens onto carcinogenetic drugs, and then perhaps anti-anti-carcinogens. Now another complication of the auto-immune question has descended upon us in the form of AIDS, or auto-immune deficiency syndrome. Is this related to our prodigal use of antibiotics or is nature trying to tell us something more?

It appears that there is no free lunch. Everything has to be paid for. Modern man's exploitation of nature has, surely, illustrated that if man still believes there is a free lunch to be had, no one can get away with it without paying. The lessons of such an attitude are now beginning to stare us in the face. But we are still planning ahead on that assumption and on the belief that we can always keep one step ahead of nature. Soon even the powerful will be forced to recognize that their power has repercussions they cannot control, and how it is self-defeating. Obviously *laissez-faire* capitalism is no answer. Neither is the sort of communism which prevails on the eastern side of the iron curtain. Both also suffer from giantism and megalomania.

In the past people like Thomas More attempted to map out a better future for all by describing an ideal state, a Utopia, but even that word is deceptive. It does not come from the Greek 'eu topos' (good or fortunate place) but from 'ou topos' (no place, nowhere). Hence William Morris' *News from Nowhere* and Samual Butler's *Erewhon* which, near enough, is 'nowhere' backwards. How does one change a fictional 'nowhere' into a real 'somewhere'?

The communism practised by primitive societies or by the early Christians in small groups did a lot of good. The exercise of property on a small scale also did little harm. Few could object to the ownership of a house with a small plot of land and the tools of one's trade. Communism on a small scale is unifying and altruistic, in which consideration for others is paramount. Communism as practised by governments is scarcely communism at all, replacing fellow feeling by mistrust and repression. So we must keep things small. Great size depersonalizes, reduces people to cyphers, to numbers in a statistic, to robots and eventually to zombies. There should be limits to size. Indeed there are optimum limits. There is an optimum limit for private endeavour and an optimum limit for co-operative endeavour. Also there is an optimum limit for national endeavour. Leopold Kohr in *The Breakdown of Nations* had some useful things to say about optimum size.

Optimum limits are natural. The balance of nature is maintained by them. Our own balance is maintained by such limits but we do not recognize it. We have become unbalanced as a natural species and have consequently put our whole world off balance. The necessity for basing human law on natural law was a prime motive in the philosophy of the Russian thinker Alexander Radischev at the time of Catherine the Great. According to J.V. Clardy's book, Radischev considered natural law as being that which conformed to the natural order of the universe and was to be found in the nature of humankind itself. He also considered that an eternal framework existed which connected all people for all time. Man and his environment, man and the universe, should obey the same laws. Such thinking reflects the philosophy before the Enlightenment when man and nature, man and the universe, were inseparable. If a model for the future of society is sought then Radischev's ideas might not be a bad starting point. However, the trouble with his observations is that their application appears to be doctrinal rather than organic. Somehow the ideal and the organic must be brought together in a kind of symbiosis. But if we take ideals as compass points, not destinations, as Lewis Mumford suggests, the immediate attainability of any goal becomes unimportant. What is important is the direction in which to go. Whether we reach the goal is another matter and, perhaps, for another age.

To change the scene we must change the minds that set the scene. It's no longer a matter for doubt that even deeply engrained assumptions and attitudes may be changed. For instance, take the revolution in the public's attitude to smoking. Dissemination of the knowledge that smoking is a killer has changed the habit of millions in a few short years. Another revolution which bids to become even speedier is in the public's attitude to sex when faced with the dread prospect of AIDS. People will change ideas and deeply engrained habits if brought up short against their disastrous consequences. Chernobyl has upset the general public's attitude to nuclear power. It has not quite convinced them yet, but a change of view is on the way. Let us hope it will not necessitate further Chernobyls to bring about such a revolution in thinking. Even acid rain and lead in petrol are now beginning to worry governments and industry. What holds the revolution back, of course, is the profit motive but even this will come to heel when it is seen that its very existence is threatened.

Another factor is the increasing part women are beginning to play in external affairs. It was Ashley Montagu who remarked that while women loved the human race, men behaved as if they were hostile to it. But women, he says, because of the sense of inferiority imposed upon them should not adopt male values and masculine characteristics or try to compete with men. Competition is a masculine vice; co-operation a feminine virtue. Neither women, nor men, should compete with the other. They should co-operate.

Competition between world powers has brought the world to the brink of disaster. Co-operation between small groups may yet save it, for above all else it will indicate a radical change of mind. It will be a decision not to kow-tow to the demands of big business, 'progress', jingoistic patriotism, and government autocracy. It will demonstrate a desire to get down to basics: the earth and our relationship with it. With such a change of mind technology would no longer be a threat, for we shall know how to use it to benefit humanity.

Our World • Your World • Their World

The earth is a small planet in the solar system and, due to technology, rapidly getting smaller. The world, on the other hand, again due to technology, is rapidly expanding. The earth is that hard, seemingly solid, round ball on which we are born, live and die. The world is our experience of everything outside us and within us. The earth is included in the world. The world is included in the earth. The earth is the realm of the tactile, the visible. The world is the realm of ideas, imagination, convention, values, language, mathematics, science and art. We are born and cradled in the earth. We give birth to the world and at the same time it gives birth to us. We are what links earth to world and world to earth through our sense organs, our mental *a priori* co-ordinates, our reasoning, our conventions, our personal experience and history, through education or indoctrination, and through our national, tribal or familial background.

The earth is natural; the world is human. Good or bad, sanity or insanity, do not apply to the earth. It is here, as it is, free of any value judgement we may apply to it. But the world, that is another matter. The world is beginning to look not only decidedly unhealthy but in terminal decline; a decline which may even bring the earth down with it.

How do we human beings fit into this world-earth framework? We are told that the sun is 93 million miles away, that enormous galaxies of stars are several light-years away, that the universe is rapidly expanding, that the universe is running down, and so on. I wonder. I wonder if they've really got it right this time. I wonder if the truth is not something quite different. For the universe that presents itself to us is of our own making. It depends for its existence on our senses. Even the most powerful and sophisticated telescopes and microscopes are but extensions of our sense of sight; the most powerful and delicate listening devices that can hear sounds from outer space or within the womb itself are but extensions of our sense of hearing. We only register what our senses can bring within their range. Are we meant to believe that this is all there is? That there is literally nothing more? Or rather, only something more of the same, for with more highly developed instruments one will no doubt see and hear more of the same.

Sir Arthur Eddington used to claim that the universe started some 90,000 million years before Christ and that its circumference was of the order of 6,000 million light-years. What, I wonder, was going on before that date, or was that the beginning of time itself? And what could lie outside its circumference? The Tao? The Demi-Urge? Surely such statistics are nonsense figures giving rise to nonsense questions, like the 'Big Bang' theory or the 'Steady State' theory, meriting a sharp rap over the knuckles from the nearest Zen Master.

How did everything begin? I do not believe in the 'Big Bang' or the 'Steady State' any more than I believe that the world was created in 4,004 BC, or that the earth is flat. The first two theories are just as much speculation as the latter were. The one sure thing about science is that it has to keep on correcting itself however much it may impress the ignorant that this time it has got it right. So what follows 'Steady State' or 'Big Bang'? Is it perhaps a pulsation, expanding and contracting like the breathing of Brahma, which I understand lasts 4,320 million years each breath?

What a different universe we would have if our sensory equipment were other than it is. Even with similar equipment there may be immense differences. Take the world of the dog, for instance. It is hard to imagine that it can see the world as we do. Grass, lamp-posts and sheep exist for it as they do for us but what can it know of the solar system or, say, the Atlantic ocean? It has its own world limited to its own equipment as we have ours. Human beings, animals, insects – all have their different worlds geared to the respective sensory equipment provided for their appreciation so that a multitude of different real worlds exists, not only according to individuals but also at various levels hierarchically according to species, genus and so on. Each world is then immediate and real for its experiencer, and real also, but less immediate, for another member of a comparable group, family or species.

Our sensory organs put us in touch with our tangible, visible world; they bring it before us; moreover, they put us into it. But our sensory world is only part of our world. It is the outer part. According to the ancient Greeks sense-data arising from the interaction of the individual with his environment were secondary, or as Democritus put it, 'bastard' qualities, while the primary or 'authentic' qualities were perceptible to the intellect. Primary qualities were independent of both individual and his environment. They formed the inner part based on the intellect and included mathematics and logic. They could be exact, while the secondary qualities varied from person to person. A mathematical proposition is either right or wrong no matter who proposes it, whereas taste may vary from one man to another.

Primary qualities deal with 'universals', secondary qualities with 'particulars'. We live, on the face of it, in a world of secondary qualities in which primary qualities appear to play only a secondary part. Our world is external to us, made up of particulars, facts, events and what we take to be solid bits of matter. Our internal world is more elusive, dependent on succession in time rather than on extension in space. Organized, it is the field of reason; unorganized, the realm of dreams. In between we have undefined territories of imagination, emotion and feeling. Science has no hold over this inner world for it is precisely this inner world which employs science as an instrument of discovery in the outer world; a discovery which, for the most part, leads to deception.

Where does one end, and the rest of the world begin? Is the sensitive envelope of one's skin the real boundary? According to Bertrand Russell one's body is as distinct from oneself as tables and chairs are. It is in fact merely a part of the material world. According to Jean-Paul Sartre it is co-extensive with the world. I take it that there is no real boundary. Our body is part of the external environment – an extension of ourselves into it. Our body is more intimately and immediately bound up with us than the rest of the environment; we cannot change it in the sense that we can change the rest by moving about in it, exchanging one immediate environment for another. The environment then becomes a loosely-linked extension of our closely-linked extension, the body. Our appreciation of it depends on the body through the organs of sense and is never quite the same for one person as for another.

We carry our environment with us when we move, for it is tied, so to speak, to our senses and any new situation is coloured by personal memory of previous situations. Our sense of touch is limited to what our skin encounters, but our sense of smell has wider limits; our hearing reaches the thunder, and our sight the stars. We are enmeshed in a network of sense-data linking the boundary of the skin with the confines of the heavens.

If we are inextricably linked with the environment as different parts of an all-embracing whole, then the way we treat others must have some effect on the environment. Equally, the way we treat the environment must have some effect on us. Our actions may produce quick returns over a short period, but in the long run are we not shooting ourselves in the

14

foot? We are, after all, part of that world which we are so busy exploiting and destroying. We and our world are one.

Our tendency to try to isolate, fragment and analyse everything, as if it were a thing apart, has been instrumental in bringing about the spoliation of nature. We forget that such isolation is impossible. A part is not just a part; it is a part of a greater whole. A heart, for instance, is a part of a whole, the body. But the heart is also a whole in itself, containing several parts – valves, chambers, arteries, muscles and so on.

Every organism can be seen as a whole embracing different parts, or as a part of a larger whole – individual – family – clan – nation. The parts are never complete separate entities but always in relationship with other parts and wholes. Nothing is ever in complete isolation. Does this not emphasize what is wrong with our present fervour for individualism?

Rampant self-interest is a cancer cell in the body-politic. The cancer spreads, for everything is interrelated and interconnected at every level, at every place and at every time. Our actions do not stop at next door. They reverberate round the world. In the ruthless jungle we have made for ourselves one man's gain may mean a loss for countless others.

Given this little ball, this earth, to play with, what do we do with it? Nature is a-moral. There is no justice in the world we are given. Justice is something to be sought. There is no equality. Equality is something to be sought. There are natural laws and there are man-made laws. Natural laws take no account of justice. It is up to human laws to bring justice and equality to men and women. It would seem, if there were any justice, that the earth and its fruits should be shared by all. However, as we all know, the earth has been plundered, bought and sold, cut up, robbed, destroyed and polluted for centuries by a relatively small minority of powerful people. They have grabbed the best for themselves, often murdering others in the process. The robber barons and marauders of antiquity acquired respectability with time but still clung to their ill-won possessions; some became ennobled and owners of vast estates. The land grabbers were succeeded by pirates, buccaneers, gold diggers, railway magnates, ship and mine owners, oil tycoons, press barons, building speculators and the like.

At the other extreme we see countless millions of the dispossessed trying, often unsuccessfully, to scratch a living from what the greedy have not yet grabbed for themselves. Millions in India, Bangladesh and Pakistan can barely exist. More millions in Africa, in Ethiopia, in Mozambique and the Sahel, reduced to little more than skin and bone, drag themselves to food distribution points organized by western charity.

But there is never enough food or charity. In Latin America there are the forgotten landless poor of Brazil and the wretched peons of Peru and Bolivia. Even in Europe we have the deprivation of inner cities, and the slum dwellers of such cities as Naples and Liverpool.

What prevents the dispossessed from sharing in the earth and its fruits? Surely, there should be enough for everyone. As Gandhi said, there is enough for everyone's need, but not for everyone's greed. One major obstacle is the law, for over the centuries many laws have been drawn up not so much to protect those who have been robbed of their birth-right, but to protect the robbers from the robbed. Laws of course, are rarely made by the dispossessed. The underlying ethic appears to be that if one can get away with it one is entitled to do just that and, having done so, to make the deed legal. Throughout the world codes of law have been drafted to legalize injustice. Further, the law is enforced by police who, almost without exception, support the 'haves' against the 'have-nots'. This applies to communist countries also.

The expropriation is carried still further by armies who provide for governments what the police provide for powerful individuals, cartels and trusts. Governments are even more greedy than tycoons. The whole of Africa was sliced up for the benefit of white nations at the expense of the blacks. British, French, Belgians, Germans, Italians, Portuguese, Spanish and Boers carved up vast tracts of land with little or no respect for tribal boundaries, customs, religious beliefs and traditions. Old and tried systems of husbandry were abandoned. The land itself, formerly farmed in small plots, was turned over from subsistence to cash crops and parcelled out into vast estates for the profit of white settlers and international companies. In some cases forests were uprooted and the whole terrain changed in character to become incipient dust-bowls. The starvation of whole peoples, which has been a grim feature of the 1980s, is no doubt due less to the inefficiency of the native inhabitants than to the ruthless rape of land perpetrated by their erstwhile rulers.

Poverty, however, has never been solely confined to what has come to be called the 'Third World'. The poor, as has been said, are always with us, even in the relatively prosperous West. In England in the nineteenth century, Dickens made those who could read aware of how those who couldn't read, lived. The first Queen Elizabeth, travelling through England was appalled and exclaimed 'the poor are everywhere'. Later in her reign her government was obliged to introduce a poor-rate. Four hundred years later the second Queen Elizabeth's government seems to be intent on bringing in a sort of poor-law. It is not a record of which any country should be proud, though nevertheless one which is only too readily forgotten.

In our own day the gulf between rich and poor appears to be widening rapidly. Take two items from the same day's newspaper. The City's new rich. Young men in their early twenties can earn £100,000 a year and more buying and selling other people's money. Then the inner-city's new poor. Poverty has increased by 50 per cent since 1979. It is estimated that nearly 11 million people now live on or below the poverty line and, it is suggested, the government deserves much of the blame. They are not news items from two different countries such as the United States and some third world nation. They both refer to this country, Britain, a contrast surely all the more obscene. The press, advertising, business and the government all beat the drum not only for more and more of everything, but also for inequality.[1]

It is assumed that those who have no money have not worked hard and are probably feckless, if not dishonest, while those who have money are assumed to be honest and hard-working. Neither assumption, of course, is necessarily true, but if you are piling up £100,000 a year in your twenties, just for shuffling other people's money around, it must be a very comforting belief.

Another factor widening the gulf between rich and poor is that salaries and wage increases are reckoned in percentages. It's a method which gives little idea of the underlying inequitability it produces. Someone in the upper salary bracket, say on an income of £40,000, given an increase of 5 per cent gets an extra £2000 a year, or £38 a week, while someone near the bottom on £4000 gets an extra £200 a year, or just under £4 a week. At the top of the scale, in the £200,000 bracket, a 5 per cent increase means an extra £10,000 a year, or £192 a week. The annual increase is then more than double what someone at the poorer end of the scale gets as a whole wage. We are told that the rich need incentives for work and that it is good for the country. Apparently, for the less well-off, patriotism works the other way – the less they have the more they will work, and the better for the country. I admit to being a little sceptical about this theory. It doesn't appear to be working very well. Nor does the country.

But the main objection, surely, to such inequitabilities is that money brings power – power over others less-moneyed. One can't very well eat fourteen meals a day, drinks quarts of champagne or have buckets of caviar, but one can order people about and get them to do things for one. One can buy privileged treatment in a hospital, one can get the best advocacy in law courts, one can buy the best in hotels and restaurants, one can send one's children to the best schools. One can, if one wants, buy anything that is to be bought, and that seems to include practically everything nowadays. But it is no recipe for a free, fair and equitable society in which care, health, attention and education are the natural right of everyone, regardless of pay-packet or cheque-book.

The most beautiful, and at the same time the most humbling, photograph I have ever seen is that of the revolving earth taken from the moon. There on that little circling ball hundreds of thousands of miles away are we, floating and twirling in the immensity of space, for a miniscule period of some forty, sixty or eighty years, while the universe around us goes on for hundreds of thousands of years, for millions, for thousands of millions of years. Each one of us a spark extinguished almost immediately, a spark of dust in the cosmos. Should we not, in our perilous craft, all be helping each other? From the moon it looked as though that should be so. But, manifestly, it is not the case.

The more powerful have grabbed the best bits of this circling planet for themselves; the weakest can hardly exist on what is left. Not content, the powerful hurl threats and accusations from one corner of this whirling craft to the other. Millions of people are killed in wars while careering at thousands of miles an hour through space. Still not content, having reduced much of the planet to a near disaster area, even threatening to blow it up with nuclear weapons, they now want to broadcast their murderous delusions to satellites and other planets, and play at 'star wars'. The trouble is we cannot really believe it. These people do not look like what we imagine power-maniacs ought to look like. They look just like us.

At times our life-craft, the earth, appears close to shipwreck. But we do not see it like that. Nor do we act as if it were. Let us imagine a shipwreck with a boat-load of survivors. A few of the stronger survivors have put themselves in charge of all water and provisions. Days pass and the food and water get low. The survivors are rationed to less and less, but those in charge of the provisions continue to eat and drink their fill. Then day by day most of the rest fall sick and die for lack of food and water. But those in charge have not lost a stone: the provisions, they protest, are their property. Why is it that what would be considered unforgiveable conduct in a shipwreck is adjudged acceptable, even normal, when applied to this country, or to the world?

Note
1. Inequality according to Tawney diverts energy from the creation of wealth to the multiplication of luxuries. R.H. Tawney, *The Acquisitive Society,* G. Bell & Sons, 1952: 40.

Religion and Death

The fact that prophets have repeatedly told us that God is within us rather than up there, or out there, has largely been overlooked. Men have usually tended to prefer the exterior to the interior, the material to the ideal, the factual and rational to the intuitive and sensed. God, therefore, has to be in a place; heaven is a place, hell is a place, not a condition of the soul. But with the rise of science this view-point has proved increasingly difficult to maintain. The belief in God has diminished dramatically, men having transferred their belief to a more material deity – science itself, and its off-shoot technology. Women, on the other hand, have not been so easily led, for women place more trust in interior values. The Psyche, after all, has always been female. If the exterior god is male, the interior god is equally of the female gender; that is if one must sex the unsexable.

Religion, to me, is not a set of precepts – 'thou shalt' or 'thou shalt not', nor is it a collection of observances, liturgies, creeds and so on. It seems to be a strange property of the human species which, like symbolism and reason, distinguishes us from other animals. Fundamentally it appears as a sense of direction, but at a deeper level a sense of the numinous, the transcendental. Church-going and church services destroy rather than foster this sense. For me, as soon as the organ starts up the numinous departs. An empty church, however, the darker the better, sometimes seems to distil a sort of presence of which one vaguely becomes aware through some sort of sixth sense. I cannot say that I am a Christian, or a Muslim, or a Buddhist, or a member of any other religion or sect, for I take them to be variations on a fundamental theme embracing all; perhaps Aldous Huxley's *Perennial Philosophy* provides the best description of what I mean, though sometimes I veer towards a sort of pantheism. There is no sense in putting a name to it anyway. Names, laws, observances, prohibitions serve to divide what is essentially indivisible. As Lao-tzu is reported to have said: the Tao that can be named is not the true Tao.

If I felt the need to attach myself to a particular religion or sect I think I might go for the Quakers. Their lack of frills, of priests, of ceremony, indeed almost one might say of beliefs, appeals to me. They do not seem to be troubled with belief in the Virgin Birth or in transubstantiation, nor are they worried by the thought of women priests, for they have no priests. Such beliefs as they have seem to be fundamental if one is to call oneself a Christian, and beyond that nothing more is required. Peaceful people, often dedicated pacifists and conscientious objectors in wartime, supporters of CND in the nuclear debate, liberal in attitudes to sex, supporters of prison reform and advocates of good causes and lost causes everywhere, they present, in their quietist obscurity a quite distinctive portrait of British non-conformism.[1]

Most religions claim that there is something after death, while most scientists would probably say that there is nothing. What is death, and what, if anything, comes after death? Some people claim that death is but a change from one form of life to another, like the caterpillar becoming a butterfly, and that the change is for the better, the butterfly being obviously preferable to the caterpillar. In the Upanishads we read:

> Even as a caterpillar when coming to the end of a blade of grass reaches out to another blade of grass and draws itself over to it, in the same way the soul, leaving the body and unwisdom behind, reaches out to another body and draws itself over to it.

Others say that whether there is life after death or not should not occupy our minds now. Apollonius of Tyana said:

> The soul is immortal, yet that is no affair of thine, but of Providence. For thee – what profit is there in these matters? Some day, when no more, thou shalt believe it. Why then while still among the living, dost thou search out such mysteries?

This, I understand, was also the attitude of the Buddha. With death the body disintegrates, there being nothing left to animate it. But what happens to the mind, or soul?

Animula, vagula, blandula,[2]   [Bland, inconstant little soul,
Hospes, comesque corporis,   guest and companion of the body,
Quae nunc abibis in loca?   where are you off to now?]

Heraclitus of Ephesus tells us that one thing lives the death of another, that life and death are the same; the mortal is immortal, the immortal mortal. Euripides wrote: 'Who knows if this experience we call dying is not really living, and if living is not really dying?' Everlastingly the wheel turns and one thing changes into another. Life becomes death, sleeping becomes waking, young becomes old.

Is there anything in the theory of reincarnation? Pythagoras believed in it. So apparently do Buddhists who claim that many Boddhisatvas have chosen to return to earth. So it would seem did Plato if the 'Myth of Er' in *The Republic* and another passage in the *Phaedrus* are any indication. So, too, it would seem did Christ. Was he not the Messiah, born to fulfil the prophets? Did he not say 'Before Abraham was, I am'? It was not only such fathers of the Church as Cyril, Augustine, Clement and Origen who believed in reincarnation but the early Church itself largely accepted it, only later to have it anathematized in the sixth century. But what real proof have we that reincarnation is anything more than wishful thinking? Absolutely none. And why should we wish so fervently to return to this vale of tears? Have we not had enough of it? True, it could even things up a bit. The wicked who got away with it in this life would have to pay for it in the next, or the next, or the next. The blameless and the oppressed could look for something better next time. Those congenitally malformed could perhaps expect a better body the next time round, and the mentally deficient a saner mind.

With the theory of reincarnation goes the idea of 'karma', that our own actions determine our after-life, that we both judge and condemn ourselves by what we do. But without some after-life this present life must seem grossly unfair to many. In Nature to be unfair is not to be untrue; but beyond Nature it may well be. From a personal point of view I would like to have done with it. The idea of being born again, being a squalling baby again, being a teenager again does not enthrall me. But if justice is to have any meaning, then there is certainly something to be said for reincarnation.

The problem of death is linked to that of time. If time is linear and uni-directional then we can visualize birth, childhood, maturity, old age and death all stretched out one after the other in a straight line. At death we come to a full stop, with no indication of what, if anything, is to follow. All we know is that our life has run its course. But if we regard time as circular we get a different picture. When the spiral reaches death it does not stop. It continues to spiral round at a different level on which birth, childhood, maturity, old age and death mirror the first sequence, but this time on the floor above, so to speak. And so it goes on, round after round. The Pythagorean, Alcmaeon of Croton, said 'Man dies because he cannot join his end to his beginning.'[3] Parmenides remarked 'It is all one to me where I begin, for I shall come back there again.' Aristotle considered time to be circular. Nietzsche believed in 'eternal recurrence'. Even T.H. Huxley, grandfather of Julian and Aldous Huxley, believed in some form of reincarnation. Aldous had *The Tibetan Book of the Dead*[4] read to him on his death-bed. Spring, summer, autumn and winter come round again, year after year; birth and death are on each other's tails, waking and sleeping bring the day into line with the year and the life. Is waking another form of sleeping, sleeping another form of waking? Death another form of life? Does the caterpillar become a butterfly, become a caterpillar, become a butterfly?

Notes

1. During the eighteenth century the number of Quakers elected to the Royal Society was thirty times their proportion of the population. C.J. Schneer, *The Search for Order,* EUP, 1960.
2. 'The Emperor Hadrian to his Soul', Penguin Book of Latin Verse, p.61.
3. T. Gomperz, *Greek Thinkers,* vol.1; 230; Maurice Nicoll, *Living Time,* Vincent Stuart, 1952, 161; Mircea Eliade, *The Myth of the Eternal Return,* New York and London, 1955.
4. W.Y. Evans-Wentz, *The Tibetan Book of the Dead,* OUP, 1960.

Was Darwin Right?

It is still almost essential, if one wants to avoid ridicule, to believe in Darwinism. But if one lives in a 'born again' Christian community it is necessary to believe in creationism, even in Bishop Usher's inspired revelation that the world came into being in 4,004 BC, I think it was on a Thursday morning. I find it difficult to believe in almost all that is offered us on the 'when' and the 'how' of creation and descent. Even Darwin did not believe in what is now believed by many Darwinists. I have a gut feeling that none of the theories, scientific or otherwise, are right, but they are put forward with such conviction and defended with such heat that the unwary may well have difficulty in keeping an open mind. As the French physiologist Claude Bernard said, 'Theories are not true or false. They are fertile or sterile.'

Certainly some form of Darwinism could be said to be more fertile than creationism which seems to me to be completely sterile. At least Darwin provided some let-outs. And there's Lamarck with his theory of the inheritance of acquired characteristics. He believed that the individual's characteristics acquired by experience in life could be passed on to future generations. Lamarck was buried under generations of ridicule but now, it appears, may be surfacing again, albeit in a different guise.

To spread the speculative net still wider, what about Rupert Sheldrake's hypothesis of formative causation? Dr Sheldrake, a biologist, introduces a possible new factor in evolution: a 'morphogenetic field' created by members of any species into which later members of that species may 'tune'. According to him developing creatures receive a pattern-making 'transmission' from such a morphic field apart from any physical inheritance. His book, *A New Science of Life,* was reviewed by the scientific journal, *Nature,* and described as 'Infuriating . . . the best candidate for burning there has been for many years.' Looking back over the history of science one could perhaps be forgiven for regarding such a verdict as encouraging, possibly the best fillip for taking it seriously that Sheldrake could have hoped for. I admit to having been attracted to the theory if only as a reaction to rigid scientific thinking. But I wonder. Is this not also another strait-jacket in the making, for any such theory once accepted by the establishment has a tendency to turn into dogma with time? One must abandon all idea of certainty, keep an open mind, a lively curiosity and never take anything as final.

Which brings me back to Lamarck. Orthodoxy has always claimed that inheritance is through the genes which are not affected by anything acquired by an animal during its lifetime. And yet, as Professor Wood Jones has demonstrated,[1] the hair patterns on young marsupials show clearly the whorls and partings reflecting the toilet methods of their ancestors; this long before the animals have had any chance to perform their own toilet. He also claims that the 'squatting facet' on the ankle joints of Australian aboriginal infants is inherited from the habits of ancestors as they are far too young to have acquired them by their own habits. The same phenomenon has been found in the ankle bones of Punjabi babies. Another example is the 'kneeling pad' on camels which is already there on the new-born camel. Could it be that Lamarck was right, or partly right, after all? Certainly it would explain a number of things that Darwin didn't. One age's science is another age's superstition. The least we can do is to keep our options open.

Note
1. F. Wood Jones, *Habit and Heritage,* quoted by Kenneth Walker, *Life's Long Journey,* Gollancz, 1960: 86.

Complementary Pairs: Men and Women

Our world appears made up of 'twoness', polarity and complementarity
– positive and negative, rough and smooth, fast and slow, 'yang' and 'yin',
male and female. Pairs in which one half is defined by the other; indeed,
would not appear to exist without the other. Wherever one looks one
finds paired couples.

Energy, we learn, is interchangeable with matter. Indeed energy could
be regarded as an active, stretched-out, rarefied version of matter, while
matter could be seen as a condensed, inert, solidified form of energy, or as
a thickened portion of an electro-magnetic field, or as a sort of knot of
energy. Similarly, space and time form an inescapably linked pair. Matter
cannot materialize except in space; energy cannot function except in time.
Structure and function are similarly related. A structure has a certain
function. A function has a certain structure. The function is the active,
rapid aspect of the related pair, structure-function. The structure is the
passive, slow-moving, formative aspect of the accompanying function.
Each aspect modifies and informs its opposite. We live in a sort of
looking-glass world in which things only too readily appear to change
into their opposites.

According to the physicist David Bohm, mind and matter also form a
similar pair, mind being a subtle form of matter, matter a grosser form of
mind. Bohm, indeed, suggests that there is life in everything. What we
call an inanimate object has nonetheless the seed of life in it. There is no
such thing as inanimate – only various grades of animation. This seems a
nice thought and the way things appear to be going in sub-atomic physics
might even turn out to be true. It would be ironic if this resurrected tenet
of ancient Indian philosophy were to be taken up by the scientific
fraternity.

A more visible instance of paired couples, opposites, is that of men and
women. Like other such pairs of opposites they are interdependent. In a
world without women there would be no men, not just because there
would be no gestation, but because women define men, and are

themselves defined by men. Each sex is mutually essential to the existence of the other, and not only in physical terms. Each complements the other, completes the other, and balances the other. But while they may balance each other in nature, they do not in the world. The male half of the world has seen to it that the scales are tipped heavily in its favour.

I do not believe, as sociologists often seem to do, that sex differences in attitude and action are largely explainable by conventional roles assigned to each. While admitting that environment and convention certainly have a part to play, it is surely stretching credulity to suggest that genes and hormones have little or none? Males and females are different mentally and emotionally from birth, as they are physically. Role-playing may accentuate or confirm the difference or deny it, but it doesn't explain it. I don't believe the observed fact that on average boys are more numerate, girls more literate, due to role-conditioning. Or that boys are more interested in inanimate objects and their manipulation, girls more interested in people and living things. (Boys prefer motor-bikes, girls horses for example.)

It is no accident that men in general tend to be more self-assertive, women more receptive and caring for others. This does not come about through conventional patterns of thought or role-playing; it is innate. For the preservation of the race women have to care for children, men have to protect the family, the clan, the tribe, the nation. This is not role-playing but role-forming. The fact that women in general do not reach dominant positions in a male-oriented world is not a sign of inferiority but a corroboration of physical, emotional and mental differences and the demands of nature. There are, of course, exceptions – Mrs Thatcher, Mrs Gandhi, Mrs Golda Meir, for instance – but these are women with a strong masculine component who in addition have adopted male values.

That the balance between the sexes has been grossly upset is only too obvious. The world today is strongly weighted on the side of male values. Enormous sums of money are spent on weapons of war and nuclear deterrents, while the health and social services are starved. The accent always seems to be on competition and confrontation rather than on co-operation; on fighting against rather than on working with, whether one is talking of individuals or of governments.

I take it that in the beginning there were two sexes of equal value. They balanced and complemented each other, and nature saw to it that the accident of birth kept the numbers of males and females equal. What one sex lacked the other provided. They were two halves so that each could be complete only by addition of the other, corroborating Plato's myth of the origin of sex. Down the centuries, however, the balance became disturbed. The physically stronger half began to dominate the physically weaker, and the ideas of the stronger soon became paramount. Brute strength and aggression came to be seen as virtues, while tenderness and a readiness to meet others half-way came to be seen not as strengths but as weaknesses, even by the sex previously characterized by those virtues. The female sex then began to develop male characteristics and many found that this stood them in good stead with their careers. Those who achieved the highest rank in business, or especially in politics as prime ministers, became renowned for their forcefulness, aggression and ruthlessness, often outdoing their male competitors in masculine virtues.

This emphasis on physical strength, aggression and domination has spilled over into all walks of life. Weapons of war are prized, the military and police are favoured, businessmen are encouraged to be aggressive, while the poor, the sick, the very old and the very young are deprived of care and the workers of work. The male view being essentially individualistic and selfish has dominated the female view of altruism and care for others.

Technology, a product of the male mind, became an obsession and it has begun to get out of control. Those who created it do not realize how thoroughly their creation has enslaved them. The story of technology is the story of *The Sorcerer's Apprentice*; men have fathered a monster they can no longer control. Dreams of the conquest of nature, of robots, of bionic men, of travel to distant planets, even of 'star wars' begin to come real. Science fiction is on the way to becoming fact. In the meantime millions of people in the third world have died of starvation. Greed and the male view of life have conspired to render large areas of the planet uninhabitable, or centres of poverty and deprivation.

The male-female imbalance has often meant, over the centuries, that whole peoples have repeatedly been torn apart by war, in spite of the fact that the majority had no wish to fight. Today, neither the British people nor the Americans wish to slaughter the Russian people, or vice versa. Peoples of themselves would never be idiotic enough to beggar themselves or sacrifice themselves unless convinced that there was no alternative. It is governments obsessed by male values, not peoples, which bring about wars, and persuade their peoples by propaganda of the capitalist menace, or the red menace. Governments build up a climate of fear, threaten each other with annihilation, propagandize, train and discipline their compatriots, and bleed them dry to pay for their sabre-rattling. When they have gone too far, they send them to their deaths.

27

During the First World War soldiers in the trenches on both sides fraternized at Christmas – but not for long. The order came that this was forbidden; they were to get back to their lines and start killing each other again. People who had no wish to fight each other were forced to, under penalty of court-martial and possible summary execution by firing squad with the label of cowardice pinned to their shrouds. It took a brave man to fight. It also took a brave man to refuse to fight. But where was the courage of those who gave the orders? One might suggest that if women had had their way, and feminine values their due, such a war would have been unthinkable. Nothing so absurd, tragic and shameful would have happened.

This perversion of masculinity seems to be compelling, expecially when the subject of virility is in question. To take one example: it is not long since the United States suffered unbearable humiliation. The most powerful nation in the world was signally defeated in a long war by a small oriental people, the Vietnamese. It could be described as a war between helicopter-gun-ships and bicycles, and the bicycles won. The thought that an immensely powerful nation backed by the most sophisticated military technology could be defeated by a third-world people labelled derisively as 'gooks' was intolerable. The damage to America's self-image was colossal. What had happened to the proud frontiersman, the free-ranger, the pioneers of the West, let alone the United States marines? The depth of the wound no doubt goes some way towards explaining the huge box-office success of a third-rate film in which violence predominates and a loutish American hero 'Rambo' is seen returning to Vietnam, flexing his oversize biceps and pumping lead into people. Some form of masculinity, even so crude a form as this, appeared to be very much in demand. Imagination and wishful thinking were brought in to replace reality, for the reality had been too much to take; film violence might reassure the waverer that America was as virile as ever.

But not only America. Most governments of both East and West seem beset by similar fears and show similar reactions. At the beginning of this century, the British defeat by the Boers at Majuba Hill and the sieges of Ladysmith and Mafeking gave rise to similar displays of jingoism. At this moment the Soviet Union must be experiencing a comparable humiliation in its inability to subdue Afghan tribesmen, in spite of its vast preponderance of sophisticated weaponry. The emotions of fear and hate are fostered on both sides of the iron curtain. Out of them mushrooms the great build up of armaments and proliferation of nuclear weapons –

phallic symbols, assertions of virility, aggression and confrontation. The 'Macho' ideal embraces not only Reagan but Thatcher, Mitterand, and Gorbachev as well. Threats of violence on either side are never so called by the threatening government. It is always *their* aggression, *our* defence. While violence on a comparatively small scale, such as at football matches, is condemned by all, preparation for violence on a global scale is another matter; every so-called civilized country subscribes to it.

Male dominance also extends to religion, and not just in the proscription of women priests. Gods and prophets are generally of the male sex – Buddha, Jesus, Mahomet, Jehovah, the prophets of the Old Testament, and so on. The Virgin Mary and a number of Hindu goddesses do not redress the balance. The male preponderance is no doubt due to the fact that the societies which produced them were largely male-dominated. They were regarded as exterior gods, way up there in the sky, fashioned in the image of their worshippers – superman, all-powerful, all-knowing, 'the Almighty'. It was as if men were projecting their own desire for power and domination onto a vast techni-colour super-screen.

Two Extraordinary People

There are some people one can readily forget. There are others, far fewer, who leave an ineradicable mark on one's mind. One such I knew through her books; another personally.

What an extraordinary, talented and courageous woman was Simone Weil. A French-Jewish-Catholic-Socialist, a mathematician, a philosopher, a Greek scholar, a teacher, a manual worker, a trade-unionist, a mystic and, considered by some, almost a saint. At one time she worked as a factory hand in the Renault factory at Billancourt, preaching a high-powered version of socialism and idealism and became an ardent trade-unionist. She also worked as a power-press operator in an electrical factory.

But she was no uncritical socialist. She was, for instance, very critical of the leaders of the Russian revolution. Trotsky, she claimed, had never worked in a factory, and for that matter probably neither had Lenin. What could they know of the conditions of workers? She had been a brilliant student. In the entrance examination for the Ecole Normale she came top of the list with Simone de Beauvoir coming second. Later she taught philosophy and Greek. Her writing, on whatever subject, was always forthright and fearless, if also idiosyncratic and sometimes a little obscure. Her directness of speech was matched by her courage in action. In 1936 she left Paris to fight in the Spanish Civil War where, for a time, she was attached to an anarchist group supporting the government against Franco's invading forces. She was one of the first foreign volunteers.

Her religious mysticism too, like that of St Theresa of Avila, was always combined with action. In the Second World War she escaped from the Nazis and came to England. She lived in Ashford, after spending much of the war in digs in Notting Hill, London. She died in Ashford. At one time I had a bout of reading Simone Weil – *Lectures on Philosophy, Seventy Letters, The Notebooks, On Science, Necessity and the Love of God,* and latterly Sian Miles' *Anthology* published by Virago. I have been both attracted and repulsed by the writings of this extraordinary woman, but never bored.

Another remarkable character was the Rev. Michael Scott. My wife and I had got to know him through the Campaign for Nuclear Disarmament. One night he turned up at our house in Hampstead. Our daughter, who then lived only a few streets away, had sent him on to us suggesting he might find a bed for the night there. He had a toothbrush and a pair of pyjamas and stayed with us for several weeks. Michael was no conventional parson, nor did he look like one. His tall, shambling frame, a figure not unlike that of General de Gaulle, was invariably shabbily dressed for he was as careless of clothing as he was of convention. He rarely wore a dog-collar but kept one in his pocket for emergencies. His more usual get-up was a great loose sweater and a tie half way round his neck.

For an Anglican parson Michael had had an unusual career. At the age of nineteen, before becoming ordained, he had gone to South Africa to work for a mission to lepers. Following ordination he had a curacy in Sussex and another in Kensington. Later he had a parish in Lower Clapton in the East End of London. It was there, when the hunger marchers arrived, that he began to move towards the left. He read Engels' *Anti-Dühring* and Lenin's *State and Revolution.* For a brief moment he swung towards communism, but never became a card-carrying party member, and eventually disillusionment set in. This was followed by four years in India. He was mostly in Bombay and Calcutta, first as chaplain to the Bishop of Bombay, then as chaplain to the cathedral in Calcutta.

In 1940 he enlisted in the RAF and trained as air-crew; he had already qualified for a civilian pilot's licence. Invalided out of the RAF, he returned to South Africa where he vigorously opposed apartheid and racial discrimination which culminated in non-violent resistance, arrest and imprisonment. Eventually he was banned by the South African government and never permitted to return.

Moving to Namibia he took up the cause of the Herero tribe for the restitution of their tribal lands and freedom, together with the rest of Namibia, from the South African yoke. He represented the Hereros year after year at the United Nations in New York. He befriended Seretse Khama, and knew Kenneth Kaunda and Julius Nyerere intimately. Together with Mary Benson, he set up the Africa Bureau in London in a ramshackle office in Vauxhall Bridge Road, in the same building as the Anti-Slavery Society. Almost anything to do with Michael Scott was either ramshackle or a hive of activity, usually both.

Having little respect for authority the nature of his work brought him into frequent contact with it. He knew, and was friendly with, Jawarhalal

Nehru, but fell out with him over India's treatment of the Nagas. According to David Astor, he accused Nehru of putting down the Nagas with as much brutality as Britain had shown in seventeenth-century Ireland. He was even more critical of Nehru's daughter, Indira Gandhi.

On one occasion Michael persuaded me to drive him together with a Naga chief and his daughter up to Penrhyndeudraeth in North Wales to meet Bertrand Russell who had a house there. Michael was an old friend of Russell and hoped to get him to put his signature to a petition in favour of Naga self-government. But Russell declined to sign, saying that his signature was becoming devalued through putting his name to petition after petition. The journey was abortive but for an enjoyable tea and discussion with Bertrand and his fourth wife, Edith.

On 14 September 1983, Michael died, aged seventy-six. I could not believe it. Only a few weeks earlier I had met him by chance, striding along Englands Lane, Hampstead, unkempt as usual but seemingly full of vigour. A memorial service was arranged in St Martins in the Fields, addressed by Bishop Trevor Huddleston and attended by Monsignor Bruce Kent and Lord Brockway. The music was provided by Africans. It was a strange and moving occasion. There were long obituaries in *The Times* and *The Observer,* but in the popular press almost nothing.

It will not be easy to forget him. His tall, shambling figure in crumpled clothes, just as if they had been slept in, his pockets bulging with papers, his gentleness, his shyness, his wicked sense of humour and mischief, his courage, his healthy disrespect for authority, pomp and bumbledom, to say nothing of his tireless work on behalf of oppressed minorities, all mark him out from the rest of us.

Michael Scott, of course, was a subversive. He believed in non-violence and practised it, at his expense, not at the expense of others. His subversion was against the iniquities, the inequalities, the idiocies indulged in by governments and those in power. To him, Christianity meant the subversion of our normal, greedy, power-hungry and pitiless attitude to life. After all what could be more subversive than the Sermon on the Mount? Should it not be the aim of all religion to be subversive? Is not conversion the fruit of subversion?

Science and Size

Science is based on number, measure, quantity. Perhaps it was not so strange that Pythagoras became obsessed by number. He was an Ionian from the Aegean island of Samos. The Ionians were one of the three original tribes of Hellas and among them the idea of number appears to have been very strong. Like other Greeks the Ionians founded colonies. Twelve city-states were so colonized: a nice round number. The Ionians themselves were divided into four tribes. Each of these again was divided into three brotherhoods. Three, four and twelve. Three times four make twelve. The sides of the triangle in Pythagoras' theorem are in the ratio of three, four and five. Three and four make the magic number seven, while five was the number of the pentagram, the emblem of the Pythagoreans, and was also the number of the fifth perfect solid, the dodecahedron which had twelve faces. Again three, four and five add up to twelve. Enough, one would think, to soften the head. And, after all, the Pythagoreans were a bit odd. Were they not vegetarians engaged in a form of religious mysticism, and did they not allow women to their schools on equal terms with men, and that 500 years before Christ and 2500 years before Oxbridge came round to it? Even odder, Pythagoras believed in reincarnation and the 'music of the spheres'. Obviously, in these days, ripe for the psychiatrist.

In those days, however, they must have been very open-minded in Ionia for their little clutch of cities and islands in the eastern Aegean became the seed-bed of western culture, the cradle of science. There was nothing they did not question. Pythagoras' obsession with harmony and number brought him to music. Archytas tells us that he and his disciples experimented with strings of various lengths, and vessels filled with different volumes of water, as well as with wind instruments of different lengths. They noted and appreciated the relation between pitch and frequency, and they discovered the octave, the fifth and the fourth. They did not stop there: they projected their theories onto the heavens and came to the conclusion, against all common sense, that the planets

33

revolved round the sky at different speeds and distances from the centre. Their curiosity knew no bounds. Alcmaeon, a Pythagorean physician predating Hippocrates, did dissection and explored the Eustachian tube between ear and throat 2000 years before Bartolommeo Eustacchi re-explored it and gave his name to it. The Pythagoreans combined science, poetry, religion and mysticism in such a way that they can fire the imagination even to this day. Pythagoras himself could perhaps be described as the first polymath. Music, mathematics, science, philosophy, invention, medicine, art and politics all came within his grasp; he was also a politician and artist, designing the coinage of the city of Croton over which he held sway. To Pythagoras even Leonardo must cede pride of place.

Pythagoras, however, was only one of many. The genius of Ionia welled up in many places and took many forms. The island of Chios gave birth to Homer. The city of Miletus fathered Thales, Anaximander, Anaximenes and Leucippus. Leucippus, Anaxagoras of Clazomenae and Epicurus of Samos laid the foundations of atomic theory taken up and developed by Democritus. Aristarchus of Samos claimed that the earth revolved around the sun while rotating on its own axis, 1800 years before Copernicus. Heraclitus of Ephesus fathered the doctrine of the tension of opposites and the running over of one opposite into the other (enantiodromia – a variation of the Chinese Yang-Yin). It influenced C.G. Jung, and laid the ground for the 'dialectic' later to be developed by Hegel and Marx. Heraclitus also developed a theory of perpetual change which impressed Plato. Finally we have Hippocrates of Cos to whom western medicine became indebted for centuries. Ionians all.

We've come to the question of size. Those tiny islands of the Aegean and cities of Asia Minor produced such a galaxy of talent as has not been equalled since, measured against size and population. Quality would appear to have little relation to quantity. The flowering of the Renaissance in Italy took place in a few cities of Tuscany while the great period of music in Germany occurred when Germany was not a nation, but a collection of small states and principalities.

The enormous countries, the vast cities and conurbations of the present day have produced, surely, nothing comparable? We seem to be suffering nowadays from a bad epidemic of megalomania. London, not so long ago, was the largest city in the world. It is now way down the list surpassed in population by Tokyo, Moscow, and a dozen others. Now Tokyo has been overtaken. Mexico City, one reads, has a population of some 19 million while Sao Paolo is not far behind. Vast office blocks arise; great motorways are constructed with longer, more stupendous bridges and tunnels; people live in enormous tower blocks like battery hens; huge airports for jumbo-jets eat up inordinate acreages of farming land. People are distanced from people by such immensities. The concrete eats into their souls; the very size numbs their minds. They become alienated, disoriented, restless and violent, or apathetic zombies.

The feeling for proportion, for appropriate size, which meant so much to the ancients and lasted up to, say, the eighteenth century, now seems to have left us. We have become slaves to giantism. Things are valued more for their sheer size and cost than for their intrinsic worth. Plato recognized that there was such a thing as optimum size, though his estimate for a city would seem ridiculously small to us now. Nevertheless a city of 500,000 should surely be enough to provide all the intellectual and artistic stimulus for us today. Athens and Florence managed on much less. Nineteen million is a monstrosity.

With size we can bracket speed. Speed is almost as crippling to culture as size. From pre-historic times right up to the nineteenth century no one was able to exceed the speed of the horse. Then came the steam-engine followed by the motor-car, the aeroplane and now the rocket. All within 100 years. Speed is addictive, like heroin. Once it has got you it is difficult to regain control – you want more and more of it. The advertising fraternity know this only too well and not only attempt but succeed in luring buyers with cars capable of speeds of well over 100 miles an hour when the maximum permitted speed is seventy.

The speed of travel is matched by the speed of calculation. Electronic computers achieve prodigious results within seconds. Computers, too, are addictive. Moreover they appear to be very ephemeral, each new computer becoming rapidly superseded by a more sophisticated model so that it is difficult to keep up with the changes. In the short, hectic life of computerdom the first computers are already museum-pieces. Nevertheless one gets to think they can solve everything in a trice. Unfortunately they leave little time to wonder. As Schopenhauer said: 'Where counting begins, understanding stops.' Even more so with the computer.

How can we control this mania for speed or get out of the clutches of the megalomaniac monster that we have so grown to love? Happily there are signs that our love may be already beginning to wane. People like Fritz Schumacher with his books *Small is Beautiful* and *A Guide for the Perplexed,* Barbara Ward with *Progress for a Small Planet* and Leopold Kohr with *The Breakdown of Nations* are leading the way to a saner view of what life on earth could be like. It is a small beginning, but all new beginnings are small. There is a long way to go, but at least we have a start.

35

Order and Disorder

If one believes that life on earth arrived by accident, by a chance assembly of elements in a primeval slime, how does one account for the following? How does order arrive by chance out of disorder? As D'Arcy Thompson has pointed out in his book *On Growth and Form,* why should leaves of plants spiral round the stem in a logarithmic spiral, and why should the numbers of petals on a flower correspond to the Fibonacci Series in mathematics?[1] Why should the curves of tooth and claw, of animals' horns, of elephant tusks, or the spiral of the shell of the Nautilus, also conform to the curves of the logarithmic spiral? And, reaching out to the heavens, why should the spiral nebulae or galaxies also follow the logarithmic form? As Galileo suggested, it looks as if 'God geometrizes'. Again why should such curious natural regularities relate also to a Platonic solid, the dodecahedron, each plane of which forms a pentagon, which again is related to the Fibonacci Series, and also the Golden Section or Divine Proportion? The Golden Section ratio (1:1.618034) occurs over and over again in nature. Why? It seems more likely that 20,000 monkeys would in a thousand years write all the works of Shakespeare than that the primeval slime should, by accident, throw up a human being. Design is, to many scientists, still a dirty word, but if chance is absurd what other word have we?

Cosmos – the word means order as well as universe. Kosmetos in Greek means well-arranged, hence our word cosmetics. If the arrangement is not always obvious we can nevertheless catch a glimpse of it wherever we look. Take, for instance, the hexagonal symmetry of the cells in a honeycomb and then read Kepler on *The Six Cornered Snowflake.*[2] Chance? It is unbelievable. I am not saying that there is no such thing as chance, merely that chance itself is not the answer. There must be something more.

Pattern is everywhere – not just a pattern of existence, but a pattern of development. We do not develop haphazardly. A pattern is encoded in our genes. We develop along certain paths mapped out for us by such codes. The biologist Waddington claims that bodies develop along time trajectories which he calls 'Chreodes'. Such developmental paths attract to themselves a certain environment which again possesses its own particular pattern. Heredity and environment mutually interact at every stage. We are presented with an immense dynamic web of interconnecting, interlocking, interacting patterns. Such formative paths are no new idea. Kepler believed in a *'facultas formatrix'*,[3] Galen in a *'Dynamis diaplastike'* or formative power, and going back still further we have the vital fields of etheric energy patterns of Indian philosophy. Kepler, when he wrote his *De Nive Sexangula* on the snowflake did not, of course, know that the outward hexagonal form of a snowflake corresponded with the internal arrangements of the atoms which compose it, but how excited he would have been had he known it.

In his *Metamorphose der Tiere* (Metamorphosis of Animals) Goethe wrote: 'Every animal is an end in itself . . . . All limbs develop according to eternal laws.' Our bodies are fluid, changing from day to day, month to month. Cells die and are rejected, while others take their place. After a time, usually given as about seven years, our bodies have changed completely. There is not a single cell in the whole body which has not been replaced (except brain cells). Nothing of us is as it was. The eyes, the nose, the skin that marked us out before are now no more. In Plato's *Symposium,* Diotima says to Socrates:

> Even during the period for which any living being is said to live and retain his identity – as a man, for example, is called the same man from boyhood to old age – he does not in fact retain the same attributes, although he is called the same person; he is always becoming a new being and undergoing a process of loss and reparation, which affects his hair, his flesh, his bones, his blood, and his whole body.

Heraclitus of Ephesus said that one could never step into the same river twice, for it had flowed on. We can never step into the same body twice either, for it too has changed. And yet we have the impression that we are still the same person. What is it that persists in seeing the different as the same? What is it ensures that the new cells play exactly the same part as the old cells did, that they know where to go, that they know their job? It can't be part of the body for the body has changed. It can't be part of the mind for that has changed too, though memory might be thought to have something to do with it. It appears as if everyone is endowed with a sort of blue-print, a pattern of development, which the cells can read and follow, and that pattern is supplied with an identity, an 'I' which one can recognize as oneself.

Chance also seems to play little part in the following. In Jules Fabre's book *Souvenirs Entomologiques*[4] there is an account of certain wasps which can paralyze spiders, beetles and caterpillars with their sting, without killing them, in order to lay their eggs in them. The stinging is carried out so skilfully and accurately, and is so obviously adapted to the anatomy of the nervous system of its prey, with the aim of paralyzing but not killing, that even a surgeon with a scientific knowledge of the animal's nervous system could do no better than the wasp does without any previous experience. The process of the operation is so unmistakably deliberate and objectively co-ordinated that it is quite impossible to explain as a chain-reflex, or as an accumulation of inherited experience. The paralysis is essential for the deposition of the eggs, but it must not kill for the eggs need to feed off the caterpillar. Such an illustration of teleology, of purpose, of means and ends cannot surely be written off in any way as chance. The pattern and the design are overwhelming.

We can extend our illustration of order and design still further – as far indeed as the solar system. Pythagoras believed in an ordered cosmos and more particularly in the 'music of the spheres'. To most of us nowadays this idea seems about as unscientific as one can get. And yet there are pointers indicating that it may be not quite such a far-fetched idea as it seems. Kepler, for instance, found that the angular velocities of planets at perihelion and aphelion corresponded to a musical interval. In our own day Professor Heitler, FRS,[5] has claimed that from the relationships between six planets of the solar system the whole major and minor scale can be discovered. Again the late Professor Tomaschek claimed a close harmony of revolutionary periods. For example, five Jupiter revolutions (59.3 years) correspond closely with two Saturn revolutions (58.9 years); two Uranus revolutions (168.8 years) approximate to one Neptune revolution (164.8 years), while three Neptune revolutions (494.4 years) correspond closely with two Pluto revolutions (495.4 years).

There is also a very curious relationship between certain planets and the mathematical ratio 'Pi'. Take, for instance, the sidereal revolutions of Jupiter and Mars. Jupiter (11.86 years) relates to Mars (1.88 years) multiplied by 2 Pi, thus: (1.88 × 3.1416 × 2 = 11.81 years). If we take Saturn to Mars the relationship is 5 Pi, of Mars to Moon 8 Pi, while the sidereal revolution of Mercury (87.96 days) is exactly 28 Pi, or (3.14159 ×28 = 87.9646). The sidereal period is the planet's revolution measured against the fixed stars.

If we take a planet's revolution in relation to the sun, the synodical period, we find further curiosities. The Mars period is 780 days, Venus

584 days. Mars divided by Venus comes to 1.3356 which corresponds to 4/3 (1.333) and 4/3 is a musical 'fourth'. Similarly the difference Venus – Mercury is 468 days so that Venus : Venus – Mercury is $\frac{584}{468}$ which is almost exactly 5/4 or a 'major fifth'. There are many other similar oddities, indeed one gets the impression that the Demi-Urge or Great Architect has had lots of fun working it all out. The Pythagoreans used to explain that the reason why we did not hear the music of the spheres was that our ears were not attuned to such divine frequencies.[6] The position of music in the world has occupied the minds of many. Schopenhauer considered music as quite independent of the world of phenomena, indeed completely unknown to it, and suggested that it could exist to a certain extent even if the world itself did not exist.

Closer to home. How clever of nature to decide that the muscles of the heart should be geodesic; that is to say the fibres run the shortest possible course, spirally, over the curved surface of the organ, almost as if Buckminster Fuller had had a hand in it. It is, of course, an arrangement ideally suited to its function, the rhythmic contraction of the systolic beat, some 101,000 times a day, or 370 million times a year, on and on without stopping. How beautifully structure and function collaborate in a common cause. By chance? By design?

One cannot have order without disorder for they are paired couples. They mutually define each other. Between them they split the world into Apollonian and Dionysian factions. Each has it virtues and its vices. It is relatively easy to speak about order for it is logical. It is not so easy to talk about disorder for logic plays little part in it. Yet the one is as necessary as the other. Valéry named disorder a condition of the mind's fertility. Disorder and dung are good breeding grounds. Order and sterile conditions kill the germ of an idea at birth. Great discoveries rise unbidden from the subconscious disorder of our minds, not from our reason.

Notes

1. 'Geometry has two great treasures: one is the theorem of Pythagoras; the other, the division of a line into extreme and mean ratio' (Kepler).

   The Fibonacci Series was discovered by Leonardo Pisano, the son of Bonacci (Filius Bonacci = Fi-Bonacci), who in 1202 wrote his Liber Abaci in which the series first appeared. Each term of the series after the first two is the sum of the preceding two terms, e.g. 0+1=1, 1+1=2, 1+2=3, 2+3=5, 3+5=8, 5+8=13 and so on. The series, plotted on squared paper, produces a logarithmic spiral and is related to the Golden Section ($\frac{1+\sqrt{5}}{2}$) or the 'extreme and mean ratio' in the following way:

1/1 =	1.000000	1/2 =	1.500000
2/3 =	.666667	3/5 =	.600000
5/8 =	.625000	8/13 =	.615385
13/21 =	.619048	21/34 =	.617647
34/55 =	.618182	55/89 =	.617948
89/144 =	.618056	144/233 =	.618026
	↓		↓
	.618034		.618034

Each column approaches the Gold Section 'from opposite ends' but never quite reaches it however far one takes it. The Section is also related to the fifth Platonic Solid, the Dodecahedron, and also to the Pentagram each side of which is cut by the others in the exact ratio of the Golden Section. The Section is as follows:

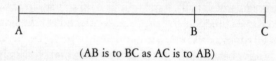

A   B   C

(AB is to BC as AC is to AB)

The properties of the above are quite extraordinary involving aesthetics, architecture, book production, plant formation, biological growth, galactic structure and music.

H.E. Huntley, *The Divine Proportion,* Dover Publications, New York, 1970: 24, 28, 46, 47, 48, 156 ff. and 164 ff; D'Arcy Thompson, *On Growth and Form,* abridged ed, Cambridge University Press, 1961: 172.

2. Johannes Kepler, 'De Nive Sexangula', 'The Six-Cornered Snowflake', ed. Colin Hardie, OUP, 1966.

3. cf. also Paracelsus' *Archaeus* and Goethe's *Gestaltung.*

4. Max Scheler, *The Nature of Sympathy,* pp.27–9, quoted from Bergson's *Creative Evolution,* 1911: 188.

5. Prof. W. Heitler FRS, *Man and Science,* Oliver & Boyd, 1963: 8.

6. Thomas Michael Schmidt, *Musik und Kosmos als Schöpfungswunder,* Verlag, Thomas Schmidt, Frankfurt, 1974. (An extraordinary book in which music, mathematics and cosmic factors are shown to be interrelated and interwoven.)

Elements and Ideas

The ancients proclaimed four natural elements – fire, air, water and earth – while we moderns claim ninety-two. The modern series starts with hydrogen and ends with uranium, plus a further group of artificial elements starting with neptunium and plutonium and ending who knows where. But the ancient elements were not so much matter as qualities, as Plato described in the *Timaeus*. They could be used to describe states of matter such as combustion (fire), rarefaction or vaporization (air), liquefaction (water) and solidification (earth). Air related to the qualities of lightness and rarity, earth to heaviness and density.

Plato's elements which came down to him from Empedocles were not, however, confined to aspects of matter; they applied also to states of mind. Allied to them were the four 'humours' – hot, cold, wet and dry – which we meet again in Aristotle and which in the forms choleric, sanguine, phlegmatic and melancholic influenced the art of medicine right up to the age of Newton. Psychologically the element fire stood for impulse and intuition, air for thought and reason, water for feeling and emotion, and earth for material perception, or sensation. Such ideas have even penetrated into modern psychology. In his *Psychological Types* C.G. Jung describes four main types – an intuitive type, a thinking type, a feeling type and a sensation type.

In the modern ninety-two elements we find irreducible elemental matter. What we have in the four ancient types or elements is a framework for thought, a set of co-ordinates and symbols which the mind can make use of to generate new ideas and clues for discovery. Such sets of co-ordinates are double-edged. If used imaginatively they can lead to new discovery, while if taken literally or rigidly they can act as a strait-jacket for thought, impeding rather than helping mental processes. Usually the latter use prevails and the framework is rejected as outworn, unscientific mumbo-jumbo.

Nevertheless the history of scientific discovery is full of the use of such co-ordinates and symbolism from Pythagoras to the *I Ching*. The *I Ching*, or *The Book of Changes,* for instance, stimulated not only Leibniz in his discovery of the calculus but also, in modern times, several Nobel laureates in physics. Leibniz, incidentally, was also much influenced by the ideas and number diagrams of the medieval Spanish mystic Ramon Lull whose scheme of knowledge employed letters, figures and symbols representing basic concepts and combinations leading, it was hoped, to the discovery of all other knowledge; it has been claimed as a fore-runner to modern symbolic logic. Symbols are multi-valent and can express, as Mircea Eliade emphasizes, several meanings at once and disclose an underlying unity to which immediate experience is blind. Symbolism and analogy are potent aids to discovery. Galileo was a master of analogy; Kepler too, admitting his indebtedness, wrote *Primum amo analogias.* Both Hume and Mill also said, in so many words, that all reasoning depends on resemblance or analogy.

The symbolism and structure in Plato's *Timaeus* first stimulated the physicist and Nobel laureate Werner Heisenberg. His father was a professor of Greek and he himself was able to read the *Timaeus* in the original. It could perhaps be described as the first astrological book ever written. That strange but universal system of symbol and structure, astrology, has had its uses. Galileo practised astrology, Kepler used it, Copernicus and Tycho Brahe were well acquainted with it, and Newton studied it.

To the unimaginative scientist, however, *The Book of Changes,* astrology, Ramon Lull and other symbol systems are nothing but examples of outworn superstition. In the scientific world of today such ideas are even less welcome than they were in the seventeenth century. They savoured too much of Pythagoreanism which was not popular in scientific circles. Galileo was accused of Pythagoreanism by the scientists of his day. Copernicus was well versed in Pythagorean ideas and found support for his theory not from the pillars of established science but from Neo-Pythagoreans, notably Giordano Bruno and Campanella. Plato's *Timaeus* was full of Pythagorean ideas and his interlocutor, the man Timaeus, was almost certainly a Pythagorean. The odd thing is that with the advent of sub-atomic and particle physics the old master seems to be coming back into his own again. Bertrand Russell's tutor, Alfred North Whitehead remarked, whereas Newton would have been nonplussed by modern atomic theory Plato would have welcomed it, and it follows, Pythagoras would have too.

Which reminds me of that much neglected genius and neo-Platonist, Nicholas of Cusa. He claimed that the earth was spherical and circled the sun in his book, *De Docta Ignorantia*[1] (Of Learned Ignorance), more than a century before Copernicus and nearly two centuries before Galileo uttered the famous 'eppur si muove' ('And yet it moves'). He too found the ancients a fruitful field for discovery. Another instance of ancient thought as a forerunner of modern discovery is described by Burnet in his *Early Greek Philosophy* where he attributes the first recorded modern type experiment to Empedocles with the klepsydra, or water-clock. He suggests that it brought him within reach of anticipating Harvey and Torricelli two thousand years later.

It would appear that essential to radical discovery is a resort to simple, basic symbols and structures. For these we have to go back to origins – the Greeks, the Chinese, the Indians. The Nobel physicist Erwin Schrödinger went back to the Upanishads. Heisenberg had discussions with the poet and mystic Rabindranath Tagore. Heisenberg himself claimed that modern science and technology had their sources in ancient philosophy and could not but benefit from classical studies. He suggested, too, that those who wanted to get to the root of things would sooner or later be bound to come across the sources of antiquity, and that their work would only benefit by learning from the Greeks how to discipline their thoughts and how to pose questions of principle. He was convinced, for instance, that Max Planck's quantum theory was influenced by his classical schooling. It prompts the thought – should we go back to teaching Greek and Latin in our schools? It seems we might do worse.

It appears that whereas a scientific education may be enough for most scientists, genius requires something more. There is considerable evidence to support the claim that the highest fliers among scientists are often not the product of education in scientific institutions like the Massachusetts Institute of Technology (MIT) or the California Institute of Technology. According to research by the Academy of Sciences and the National Science Foundation of the USA they are likely, or more likely, to come from smaller liberal-arts colleges. The Massachusetts Institute of Technology and the California Institute were not among the first twenty of the institutes which had produced the best scientists. The smaller, more intimate colleges were to the forefront.

Many top scientists have been widely read in other subjects than science, and this has almost certainly contributed to their capacity for radical discovery. However, without going into the matter too far, have we not here a warning against too much specialization in the education of our own scientists and, perhaps, a warning about optimum size? Here at least it appears that 'small is beautiful'.

The preconditions necessary for radical scientific discovery might be as follows: (1) a thorough knowledge of one's subject: there are no bricks without straw; (2) the imaginative use of analogy. As Ribot said in his well-known essay on imagination, 'The psychological mechanism of the moment of creation is very simple. It depends on one unique factor . . . thinking by analogy';[2] (3) an appropriate frame of reference; (4) an ability to combine apparently mutually incompatible ideas; (5) courage to stand out against convention and the accepted body of established theory; (6) and the time must be ripe for such a discovery.

Max Planck said in his autobiography that the pioneer in science must have a vivid intuitive imagination of new ideas, not generated by deduction, but by an artistically creative imagination. The process often seems to involve a blocked situation in which the subject, having gone over the problem again and again, comes up against a brick wall in his thinking. He lets reason drop, takes his mind out of gear, and lets the subconscious take over. He may be dreaming, absent-minded, or just not thinking about anything in particular. Suddenly, without warning, the solution breaks through into consciousness.

In the preconditions for discovery mentioned above, courage to stand out against convention is all important. How much this affected Copernicus is disclosed in his statement: 'The contempt which I had to fear because of the novelty and apparent absurdity of my view nearly induced me to abandon utterly the work I had begun.'[3] One wonders how many other radical discoveries have been lost to us for fear of being thought a crank. The last precondition is that the time must be right. In the words of Ecclesiastes: 'To everything there is a season, and a time for every purpose under the heaven.' The Pythagoreans were some 2000 years ahead of time in their thinking about the solar system, and Nicholas of Cusa about a century. Hardly anyone believed them. But the time, at last, was right for Copernicus.[4] Reluctantly the world began to accept what it had previously dismissed as crack-pot theory.

Place often tends to draw like minds together – Ionia, Tuscany, Paris – as if at the bidding of some tutelary deity. Time also seems to possess the same curious faculty. The invention of the calculus is a case in point. It occurred to both Newton and Leibniz at the same time, independently of each other. Another such time pair were John Couch Adams and Leverrier who, again independently, both discovered the planet Neptune. Michael Faraday in England and Joseph Henry in America both made their discoveries in electro-magnetism at the same time, unknown to each other. The Austrian monk Gregor Mendel and the French scientist Charles Naudin were both experimenting on hybridization at the same time, each unaware of the other. Naudin's work finally appeared in print just a year before Mendel's. In the years 1794–5 a number of evolutionary theories were in the air. Goethe in Germany, Erasmus Darwin in England and St Hilaire in France all came to similar conclusions on the origin of species fifteen years before Charles Darwin was born. Charles Darwin too had a time-twin in Alfred Russell Wallace who had come to the same conclusion on evolution, again independently. In 1925, quantum mechanics was discovered by three people, each independently of the others. There are more than a hundred other instances of independent discoveries linked by time. Indeed the phenomenon appears to be the rule rather than the exception. One might well ask, 'What is going on here?'[5] It looks as though the Zeitgeist, the spirit of the time, has considerable influence and is following Ecclesiastes to the letter.

The ability to combine apparently mutually incompatible ideas is the fourth precondition. One must be able to think not so much directly on the problem, but athwart it. Someone, I forget who, said: 'Pour inventer, il faut penser à côté,' or as Edward de Bono would put it – 'lateral thinking'. An ability to think obliquely, askew, aside from the normal seems to be a prerequisite for making any radical discovery whether we are talking of a Galileo, an Ampère or a Kékulé. Joseph Priestley, the non-conformist minister and scientist who discovered oxygen and also soda-water, claimed that he automatically took the heterodox side of every question. He was nearly lynched for supporting the French Revolution, but his heterodoxy was certainly in line with his inventive genius. Orthodoxy and invention are rare bed-fellows.

'To live in the world of ideas', said Goethe, 'is to treat the impossible as if it were possible.' To live in the world of facts is to treat the impossible as out of the question. We live in the world of facts. Genius lives in the world of ideas. The way is hard for those who 'pensent à côté', who think differently from received opinion. Socrates and Christ suffered with their lives. Roger Bacon was abhorred as a magician, Galileo was condemned by the Church, Copernicus was met with contempt, Harvey ridiculed, Descartes persecuted, and Einstein vehemently opposed.

It appears that people in any age do not like their cherished beliefs challenged any more than they like foreigners, eccentrics, the disabled, ethnic minorities or those of skin colour different from themselves. They feel unsafe. Their foundations resting no more firmly than on convention, habit, prejudice and distrust are felt to be undermined by alien ideas, distorted bodies and foreign customs. Call in the law, the police, the church, the established order before the whole world is turned on its head – save us from subversives, and since all radical discovery is in some sense subversive, save us from that too.

45

Notes

1. Nicholas Cusanus, *De Docta Ignorantia*, Eng. trans *Of Learned Ignorance*, London, Routledge.
2. T. Ribot, *Essai sur l'Imagination Creatrice*, Eng. trans *Creative Imagination*, London, Kegan Paul, 1906.
3. Copernicus quoted in *The Origins and Growth of Physical Science*, vol.1, ed. D.L. Hurd and J.J. Kipling, Pelican.
4. 'Great men are ahead, not of their time, but of their contemporaries. They cannot really advance a step further than the assumptions of the spirit of the time allow' Hermann Keyserling, *Immortality*.
5. Perhaps we could extend Dr Rupert Sheldrake's 'morphic resonance' into the realm of ideas and time. Rupert Sheldrake, *A New Science of Life*, Blond & Briggs, 1981; Paladin, 1983.

Structure and Function

Someone said, 'The greatest enemy of religion is the church,' and is there not more than a grain of truth in it? But then again if one said: 'the greatest enemies of science are scientists', would there be any truth in that? I suspect, more than a little. What about those who rejected Galileo, Copernicus or Einstein, for instance? Many scientists refused to admit Copernicus' discovery long after he died. Indeed, for three hundred years afterwards only 180 works were based on Copernicus out of over 2000 published on astronomy, the rest apparently still preferring Ptolemy.[1]

Could one go on to say that among the greatest enemies of justice are lawyers and the law? With some reason, since the law, while it pays lip service to justice, has often made sure that justice is extremely difficult to obtain if one has not the wherewithal to pay for it. Again, would it be true to say that the greatest enemy of health is the medical profession? A cynical sufferer from iatrogenic disease might well say so. Does this not come down to the point that often the greatest enemy of the function is the structure on which it depends? In Nature structure and function are in harmony, reflecting, modifying and guiding each other. In human institutions such harmony too rarely seems to be the case.

According to Montaigne[2] the art of medicine was inclined to change with the weather. In function that may well be true, especially in technology. But in structure it seems as rigid as ever. Yet not quite. There has recently been a revolt, though as yet a minor one, against some of the practices of orthodox medicine. The public, it appears, have become disenchanted with the attitude of many doctors to their patients. They object to being treated as cases – a heart case, a hiatus hernia, an arthritic hip, a prostate – rather than as a whole human being suffering from partial malfunction. The fault seems to lie partly in the prevailing reductionist view of science and the increasing availability of specialist technology. The latter is without doubt a great boon – an artificial joint for an arthritic hip, for instance. But it also brings with it considerable disadvantages, for it tends to come between doctor, or nurse, and patient, alienating one from the other.

In other walks of life – government, the army, large firms – specialists are at the behest of prime ministers, generals and managing directors. But in medicine it is the specialists who rule. And since it is in the nature of specialists to specialize, the patient becomes fragmented: separated limb from limb and organ from organ, the offending part being treated as if it had little or nothing to do with a living, breathing, probably scared human being.

In the early days of medicine things were different. The Pythagorean physician Alcmaeon of Croton investigated the nature of sense perception, the nutrition of the embryo in the womb and the physiological changes necessary for sleep. He has also been claimed as the founder of empirical psychology. But whatever he investigated he always had in mind the whole person, and held that what preserved health was a balance of the physiological functions. Everything had to be taken into consideration, the parts and the whole in mutual reciprocity. A generation or two later Hippocrates also took a holistic view, even bringing in the environment, as his *On Airs, Waters and Places* testifies. Another ancient system of medicine, Chinese acupuncture, also emphasized the whole person.

In the sixteenth century, Paracelsus, and in the nineteenth, Hahnemann, who originated homoeopathy, both stressed the importance of treating people as integrated wholes, rather than as assemblies of separate parts. Now we see a re-awakening of interest in acupuncture and homoeopathy, both of which had until recently suffered as objects of ridicule by orthodox medicine. The scene has opened up still further with other 'alternative' therapies from osteopathy to herbalism, from biofeedback to naturopathy, from colour therapy to reflexology. As long as the practitioners are well-trained and competent it can only be a good thing. There is more than one way of looking at health and disease. Why should one view point monopolize the field and attempt to deny it to others?

Alternative medicine may be on the increase but it is still, in general, restricted to those who can afford it. Those who cannot have to settle for the orthodox. If only the state would embrace the unorthodox also. Governments make great play with 'freedom of choice', yet restrict that freedom to the size of one's cheque book. In a really free society it is not only medicine that should admit more than a rigid orthodoxy but education and even law. Private schools have some latitude for experiment but state schools little – again the cheque book. Governments should provide for some form of alternative education, a few experimental schools not tied to money. Educationists should be given the opportunity and the wherewithal to start up alternative schools provided they can produce evidence of competence and character. Such schools would not endanger the conventional sort. People are generally conservative and only a minority would wish to avail themselves of this added freedom. But such schools might well act as a stimulus to the more orthodox, prevent their ossification and open up new approaches to education.

The law is a more difficult problem, for one cannot very well have alternative law. Even if the law is an ass it is nevertheless the law of the land. But the operation of the law is another matter. If has often been said, not without reason, that as far as the operation goes there is one law for the rich and another for the poor. Could we not, for a start, have alternative forms of advocacy? Already in some courts a lay-advocacy service has been permitted. It has succeeded in giving valuable help to clients who, for reasons of their rights or lack of money, have had no other representation. But even a lay-advocacy service cannot operate without some financial support, nor can it extend its activities to cover all who stand in need of it. The legal-aid scheme was a step in the right direction but many who have come before the courts are not covered by it and, as well as being chronically short of money, it has recently suffered a further battering from the government. In any event, why should not every orthodoxy be saddled with an unorthodox gad-fly on its back to prevent it becoming moribund?

Things cannot, of course, function without some sort of structure. The mind naturally tries to impose structure as part of its function, as with Aristotle. Karl Popper claims that animal behaviour and structure are biological analogues of theories, and that theories correspond to bodily organs in their method of function. Organs and behaviour, he says, are 'tentative adaptations' to the world, as are theories. Both, in their separate ways, bring influence to bear on the world and help to change it.[3]

Structure provides us with sets of co-ordinates for our orientation which help us to make sense of a confusing world. Combined with symbolism, structure provides a framework by means of which we can relate mind, body and world in a meaningful way. Just as there are three dimensions of space, there are also three directions – vertical, longitudinal and lateral. The vertical points upwards and downwards, the longitudinal points forwards and backwards, while the lateral points sideways to right and left. On the human body they would run head to feet, chest to back, and side to side, respectively. On these axes at right angles to each other we can plot ideas, for each pole is associated with a category of meaning peculiar to itself.

With the vertical axis we associate ideas of good and evil, up and down, superior and inferior, ideas of hierarchy and class, parent and child, origin and end, and such emotions as hope and despair. On the longitudinal axis, forward and backward, we have progress and reaction, anticipation and memory, future and past. On the latitudinal (lateral) axis we have right and left with an emphasis on balance, equality and complementarity, such as in male–female, husband–wife, equal partners. Some ideas will be seen to fit somewhere between two axes rather than on one.

These three diameters relate to the three 'great circles', the co-ordinates which describe the position of the earth in space – the meridian, the horizon and the prime vertical. Two of these, the meridian and horizon, have had significant importance in structuring human history. Ernst Cassirer[4] in his *Philosophy of Symbolic Forms* points out that the intersection of these two diameters (called by the Romans *'decumanus'* and *'cardo'*), formed the first basis for a scheme of co-ordinates in religious thinking, and their influence spread to almost every branch of rational thought.

As with Pythagorean number in physics, and the 'golden' section in architecture, the influence of the meridian and horizon penetrated deeply into people's minds. Roman camps, Italian cities, and even the ground-plan of the Roman house were planned with the intersection of these two diameters. Temples and cathedrals were also thus oriented. Even the law and theoretical science were to become influenced by such co-ordinates. Compare this, too, with the meridians of acupuncture on whose threads, according to the Chinese, all our diseases are strung. Number and structure run right through us from top to bottom, from front to back, from side to side, from birth to death.

With the division of the circle into four, into eight and into twelve, the range of meaning and relation is enormously increased. We find the duodecimal structure in the clock and the measurement of time, the octaval in the compass and the orientation of space. The duodecimal also became the basis of memory systems in the Renaissance, and it turned up, too, in Kant's twelve 'categories' and 'judgments.' It is as though we find it difficult to think straight without such structures to guide us, as though they were graven indelibly on the human mind as part of a background to all *a priori* judgement. Kepler, indeed, believed that the soul contained within itself that twelve-fold figure – the zodiac. Numbers, forms, structures, symbols and archetypes help us to make some sense of an otherwise rather incoherent world.

One application of structure to the human condition is the art of categorizing. It goes back a long way, at least to Theophrastus. In modern times Schiller split people into 'realists' and 'idealists', while in *The Birth of Tragedy* Friedrich Nietzsche elaborated two contrasting types, the 'Apollonian' and the 'Dionysian', the former being calm and rational, the latter restless and irrational. Another division into 'Classical' and 'Romantic' likened the Classical to the Apollonian, the Romantic to the Dionysian. Similarly we can pair 'static' against 'dynamic', 'orderly' against 'chaotic'. In Chinese philosophy Confucianism obviously fits into the Apollonian box, Taoism into the Dionysian. Similary in poetry we could describe Milton as Apollonian, Blake as Dionysian. In music Bach is more Apollonian, Beethoven more Dionysian or Romantic. Such dichotomies are further reflected in William James' 'tender-minded' and 'tough-minded', C.G. Jung's 'extra-version' and 'intro-version', and Kretschmer's 'cyclothyme' and 'schizothyme'.

Division into threes and fours is obviously possible, also. In the nineteenth century Alexander Bain divided people into 'intellectual', 'emotional' and 'volitional', or intellectual, artistic and practical types, while in the twentieth century William Sheldon partitioned his types into 'cerebrotonic', 'viscerotonic' and 'somatotonic'. When we come to fours, we have Hippocrates' sanguine, melancholic, choleric and phlegmatic compared with Jung's thinking type, sensation type, intuitive type and feeling type. Behind such dichotomies, trichotomies and tetrachotomies lay, of course, the twelve-fold character-system of the zodiac which maintained its influence from the earliest times right up to the Age of the Enlightenment.

The trouble with such a system is that one tends to take it to the letter. If a person does not quite conform to a type the tendency is to stretch or truncate him to fit the Procrustean bed; and having done that as well as labelled him, one continues to read the label rather than the individual for ever after. The desire to simplify, pin down and stereotype what is essentially complicated and fluid is too tempting.

Theoretical structures are one thing, living structures another. A living structure, say bone, is not the hard, rigid substance it appears to be at first sight. It is worked upon by function, by muscle, by time. Gradually it grows, changes form and disintegrates. Similarly function is governed by the type of structure it serves. In the same way our mental structures are not, or should not be, rigid, immutable categories. They are guides, pointers to understanding. Bone and muscle modify each other. So do, or should do, reason and imagination.

51

Notes

1. See G. de Santillana, *The Crime of Galileo,* Chicago, 1955: 164 n. quoted by Michael Polanyi, *Personal Knowledge, Towards a Post-Critical Philosophy,* Routledge, 1958: 147.
2. Montaigne, *Essais,* vol.5, chap.XIII: 217.
3. Karl Popper, *Objective Knowledge,* p.145, quoted by Brian Magee, *Popper* Fontana, p.65.
4. E. Cassirer, *The Philosophy of Symbolic Forms,* vol.I, New Haven, Yale University Press, 1965.

'In the Beginning was the Word'

Our world would not be as it is without words. We could not describe it. We could not understand it. A major factor separating us from other animals is speech, and for speech one needs words. It is true one can make oneself understood to a limited extent by gesture, but without words one is soon brought to a halt. Speaking is our way of uttering thoughts. Words are the building bricks of communication.

When we speak the sound comes out through the mouth and back in again through the ears. It is both outward and objective as well as inward and subjective. Von Humboldt[1] says the idea is translated into true objectivity without being withdrawn from subjectivity. Without this, he claims, the formation of concepts would be impossible. Something similar seems to occur with gesture in the movements of small children, where ineffectual clutching or grasping is succeeded by pointing. Here the clutching is inward and subjective, the pointing outward and objective. Cassirer tells us that words of saying are derived from verbs of showing, at least in Indo-Germanic languages. An example is the Latin word 'dicere' to say, which stems from the Greek root 'deiknumi' to show.

In speech the inward/outward aspects are often expressed by the letters used. The letters 'm' and 'n' indicate an inward direction, while pointing outwards falls to the more explosive 'b' and 'p', 'd' and 't', 'k' and 'g'. According to Cassirer, Indo-Germanic, Semitic and Ural-Altaic languages show a remarkable similarity in this respect. Note the letter 'm' in the words mother, Mutter, mère, madre, mētēr and mater, in English, German, French, Spanish, Greek and Latin respectively. Also the diminutive 'mamma' and 'mum', while the 'n' is found in 'nanny' and 'nurse', all indicating a receptive, subjective attitude. In constrast the more explosive consonants are found in father: Vater, père, padre, pater, and the diminutives pappa, dad and pop. The Indian words for mother and father are 'man' and 'bap', the former suggesting an inward embracing movement, the latter an outward thrusting into the world.

53

As for gesture, the inward/outward aspect of limb movement is notable and moreover is affected by our relation to colour. Merleau-Ponty in *The Phenomenology of Perception* tells us that red and yellow favour abduction (stretching outward) while blue and green encourage adduction (pulling in towards the body). In the art of acupuncture the meridians follow either outer/extensor/abductor aspects of limbs, or inner/flexor/adductor aspects, reflecting the Chinese concept of yang and yin. The inner/yin, outer/yang is also demonstrated physiologically in the sensory/motor nerve conduction in the limb. In the arm, the yang aspect is motor, outwards, from the brain to the muscles of arm, hand and fingers. The message goes out from centre to periphery. The yin aspect is sensory, inwards, from the skin surfaces of the hand and arm back to the brain. Mentally the former relates to the logical method of deduction (general to particular), the latter to induction (particular to general). The connecting threads running through this rag-bag of observations may seem slender, but if we think about it are we not left with the idea of an underlying co-operation of structure, function and meaning which permeates our whole existence?

Words are less than precise instruments for conveying meaning. A word, though more precise than a symbol, nevertheless carries a variety of interpretations. What, for instance, do we mean by the word 'cause'? Aristotle presents us with four different kinds of cause – formal, efficient, material and final. Which do we mean when we use the word? Take again the word 'feeling', a hydra-headed monster with a multitude of nuances. Scheler[2] distinguishes the following: fellow-feeling (Mitgefühl), projective 'in-feeling' (Einfühlung), contagion (Gefühlsansteckung) and genuine participation (Einsfühlung). We can say that the context in which the word is used defines the meaning. But the context is not the same for everyone, for the context embraces what we ourselves bring to its understanding.

The trouble with words is that they do not come to us new-minted. They are already swathed in associations, battered by history and twisted by misuse when we get them, and such accretions stick to them however careful we are in their use. Suppose we look at the word 'superstition'. My dictionary describes superstition as a false, misdirected belief based on ignorance. Superstition is set against reason and common-sense and carries with it a markedly pejorative flavour. Yet for centuries it was not superstition, but reason and common-sense that told people that the earth was flat. Only the superstitious Pythagoreans thought otherwise and were ridiculed for it. As Bertrand Russell remarked, it was not the most rational of the Greeks who made the greatest contribution to science; it was the Pythagoreans who combined science with mysticism. The Latin word *superstitiosus* has also the meaning 'prophetical' which surely describes the Pythagoreans better than their more orthodox flat-earth critics. To Goethe superstition was the poetry of life.

Another much misused word is 'myth'. In common speech it is used to mean something untrue. It has become, in effect, a sort of smear word. One has only to say something is a myth to deny it any validity. But as Malinowski says, myth is a vital ingredient of human civilization, not an idle tale. It is a hard-working active force, a charter of primitive faith and moral wisdom. Mircea Eliade and Robert Graves would surely agree. Myth fulfils a necessary function in primitive culture as regulator of belief, sustainer of morality and prescriber of rules for guidance.

Communication between human beings originated with speech and gesture. Such communication was instantaneous and ephemeral. Duration and permanence were only achieved by finding some means of recording the import of our grunts, cries and gibberings. The Egyptians evolved a form of picture writing – the hieroglyphs, or sacred writing, as it was originally confined to the priesthood. The Sumerians developed a wedge-shaped cunei-form script. Later cultures invented a series of signs or marks – an alphabet – partly pictographic, partly reminiscent of the cunei-form. We can trace our alphabet back to the Phoenicians through the Greeks and Romans. The first four letters – the Greek alpha, beta, gamma and delta – are related to the Hebrew aleph, beth, gimel, daleth (ox, house, camel, tent). Indeed the alpha upturned V is reminiscent of an ox with horns, the beta of a house with two stories, and the delta Δ of a tent. The German for delta (Zelt) means tent. Gamma, however, has little resemblance to a camel though the word gimel certainly has.

It is claimed that our alphabet originated at Byblos in Phoenicia, in what is now Lebanon. Byblos in Greek meant 'papyrus' from which paper was made and it later came to mean 'book', hence 'bible' and 'bibliography'. Originally, sentences were written from right to left as in semitic languages. But the Greeks, ever experimenters, began to switch from side to side, one line right to left, the next line left to right and back again like ploughing a field. It was called 'boustrophedon' or 'ox-turning' writing. Finally the Greeks settled for left to right, and so it has come down to us.

In western languages meaning is linear, succedent in time. Chinese has no alphabet but pictograms, and the meaning while necessarily succedent in time is more immediate, as looking at a picture is more immediate than reading a book. The Chinese language is monosyllabic and its pictograms are often stylized versions of pictures of things or combinations of such pictures. The difference between Western and Chinese ways of thinking is demonstrated in the way meaning is approached. No doubt the puzzling 'inscrutability' of the Chinese to western minds is due to insufficient appreciation of the way they think. In the West meaning is linear, logical, sequential. In the East it is more 'circular', intuitive, immediate. It is the difference between the technician and the artist.

It appears, if the linguistic researcher Noam Chomsky is to be believed, that the structure of language is to some extent innate. It too is interwoven in the complicated mesh of our body-world complex. But in language the framework of grammar seems to get less complicated as it develops. Latin grammar, for instance, is more complicated than its Italian, Spanish or French successors. In primitive languages the grammar is often extremely involved and cumbersome. In Ki-Swahili, for example, which is a Bantu tongue, there are ten different classes of noun, and adjectives have to agree with each class respectively. To confound matters still further verbs have peculiar tenses. There is, for example, a 'not yet' tense, and an 'even should' tense, a 'though' tense and an 'always' tense.

As languages evolve they seem to free themselves from a lot of excess grammar. English, a forked tongue culled happily from two main roots – Latin and Germanic – has succeeded in doing away with cases and gender. French has rid itself of the former, but kept gender. German not only keeps masculine and feminine, but also neuter, and hangs on to the rudiments of case as well. English appears to have developed the furthest. It is more flexible and has a larger vocabulary. It is also the most widely spoken language of any, though with the lack of rational coherence between spelling and pronunciation it is, in this respect, poorly equipped. Evolution usually means greater complication; in language this appears to apply only to vocabulary, not to structure.

The French Existentialist writer, Merleau-Ponty[3] regarded speech and thought as 'intervolved', the sense being contained within the word, and the word being 'the external existence of the sense'. We intuit before we can find words to describe our intuition. When we do find the words, reason constructs a framework of meaning within which our intuition is contained. This framework, constructed out of language, can now be understood by others. We can get across what we could not with pure intuition. But the framework to some extent distorts the original, for words are clumsy instruments and bruise and twist the meaning in the process. No word can ever be exact for the intention of either speaker or writer; it inevitably carries with it a lot of baggage which could well be done without. The sense, the original intuition, may come through but only in the form permitted by its mid-wife, the word. The art of writing is to minimize the malformation of an idea by choosing the most apt word.

I have always been interested in the origin and derivation of words. The French verb, 'se coucher', for instance, has its origin in the Vulgar Latin, 'se collocare', which means to settle oneself, to lie down, to settle in property or to settle in marriage. 'Collocatio' meant 'a giving in marriage'. This seems to go a little further than 'se coucher' would appear to do. The word 'coward' has curious connotations. It comes from the French 'couard' which meant one who dropped his tail. In heraldry a 'lion couard' meant a lion with his tail between his legs, the dropped tail indicating cowardice. 'Couard' came from old French 'coue', from Latin 'cauda' a tail. The same occurs in Italian where 'codardo' a coward comes from 'coda' a tail and again back to 'cauda'. A coward was, in effect, one who turned tail and ran.

It is not a matter of common knowledge that the words Church (Eng.), Kirk (Scot.), Kirche (Germ.) and Kerk (Dutch), all derive from the Greek 'Kyriakon Doma' meaning the 'House of the Lord'. 'Kyriakon' is connected with the Greek 'Kyros' meaning 'supreme power', or 'lord', and 'Kyros' in turn is derived from Sanskrit 'Çura', a 'hero'. The French for church, 'Eglise', on the other hand, comes from the Greek 'Ekklesia' meaning an 'assembly'. 'Ekklesia' also gives us our word 'ecclesiastic'. A history of events is complemented by a history of language which can provide us with a further insight into how events occurred since it is only through language that we know anything at all.

The durability of words and phrases is unpredictable. The Celtic influence, one would have thought, disappeared from the language of the English some centuries ago. Yet in Lincolnshire people still, or did until recently, count sheep in fields, and stitches in knitting, in a very un-English way: 'Yan, tan, tethera, pethera, pimp' (one, two, three, four, five); 'sethera, lethera, hovera, covera, dik' (six to ten); 'yan-a-dik, tan-a-dik . . . bumpit' (elevent to fifteen); 'yan-a-bumpit, tan-a-bumpit . . . figitt' (sixteen to twenty). The Celtic connection is evident in, for instance, 'pethera' (Welsh 'pedwar') 'pimp' (Welsh 'pump'), 'dik' (Welsh 'deg') and 'tan-a-dik' (Welsh 'dau-un-de'). 'Bumpit' too is obviously related to Welsh 'pymtheg'.

The Normans have left us an unmistakable heritage in words like beef, mutton and pork. The Romans, although they don't appear to have made much of a mark on such basic matters as husbandry and knitting, made up for it in the law and medicine by providing us with the roots of nearly half the English language. The common people, however, under Norman rule must have spoken little French and under the Romans even less Latin.

The French word boutique is much in vogue nowadays in this nation of shopkeepers – 'une nation boutiquière' as Napoleon dubbed us. Boutique is connected with 'bodega' (Span.), 'bottega' (Ital.), 'booth' (Eng.), and 'buth' (Icelandic). One would never guess that it had any Greek connection, but it has. It has come, with much twisting and turning over the years, from the Greek 'Apotheke', meaning a storehouse.

The word 'dilettante' is, of course, anglicized Italian which means literally one who delights in something or a variety of things. It comes from the Latin 'delectare' to delight, and is roughly equivalent to the word 'amateur' in its best sense: 'amateur' meaning 'admirer' or 'one who loves' from the Latin 'amator'. Leonardo had more than a dash of the dilettante in him. So did Goethe. The Renaissance was full of dilettantes. Nowadays the word is confined to someone who plays around without taking anything seriously. There are many words we take for granted without looking too closely at what they might mean. Objectivity is such a word. Objectivity and subjectivity are put to us as if they were equal and opposite concepts. But objectivity is impossible for us. It is not in our nature. It is relative and dependent on subjectivity. To say a person is objective in his judgement is merely to say he is less subjective than one would expect. Another slippery word is 'fact'. What, one might think, could be more solid or irrefutable than a fact? But what we call a fact is dependent on our frame of reference, our conceptual system and convention, which determine it. These are not added later but partake in the definition of the fact itself, right from the beginning. As Goethe said, 'The best would be to understand that everything factual is already theory.'

The word 'love' like the word 'feeling' has many nuances of meaning. The Greeks had at least three words for it – 'Erõs' (physical love), 'Philia' (love between members of a family or friends), and 'Agapē' (love that is all-embracing, for which today the word 'charity' is no equivalent). In these days, as ever, Erõs is very popular, Philia perhaps less so, while Agapē is barely recognized. It was, of course, Agapē that St Paul described in *Corinthians*. It could perhaps best be characterized in the words of William Law:

> By love I do not mean any natural tenderness, which is more or less in people according to their constitution; but I mean a larger principle of the soul, founded in reason and piety, which makes us tender, kind and gentle to all our fellow creatures . . .

Another word much ill-used and bruised in the handling is 'patriotism'. It has connotations ranging from the flagrant jingoism of the armchair warrior to the final self-sacrificing action of one who lays down his life for his country. Dr Johnson was so disgusted with the misuse of the word that he described patriotism as the last refuge of the scoundrel. Nowadays it appears it might often be described as the prerogative of the well-off. It is a word rarely heard amongst the poor. Indeed patriotism does, not infrequently, seem to be closely linked with money. Beat the drum and wave the flag, but put your money in a tax-free haven like the Cayman Islands. Patriotism is a word much loved and much misused by the gutter-press. 'The more bigoted the jingo, the greater the patriot' seems to be their motto.

Language may be an instrument of communication and understanding, but at the same time it is a trap. By the process in which we spin language out of our own being, we ensnare ourselves in it. As von Humboldt says, each language draws a magic circle round the people to whom it belongs. It is at once a prison and a liberator.

Brevity, we are told, is the soul of wit and many writers manage to encompass much within a small space.

> It is better not to say anything at great length but to leave some things for the reader to guess at and to find for himself. The reader who has guessed what was left unsaid becomes a collaborator and friend. The writer who has said all demeans your intelligence.

So said Plato's pupil, Theophrastus. 'Quidquid praecipies, esto brevis' (Whatever you teach, be brief), wrote Horace. Poetry is one way of compressing much within little. The German word for poetry – 'Dichtung' – emphasizes this. 'Dicht' means 'thick' so that 'dichtung' also means thickening, close-packing, condensation, and indeed poetry does close-pack meaning. The most striking example here is perhaps the Japanese 'haiku' which expresses the infinite in the finite in seventeen syllables.

But beyond poetry there are many examples of writers accomplishing much within little. Ludwig Wittgenstein's famous *Tractatus,* for instance, can be read in an hour or so, though it takes rather longer to understand it. The *Tao-teh-Ching* and Plato's *Crito* are short enough. Machiavelli did not waste words, either. In my copy of his *Il Principe* the first chapter occupies merely twelve lines, though followed by two pages of notes. The second chapter is half a page, the third manages eight pages, but the whole book of twenty-six chapters only occupies 146 pages, of which almost half are notes. Some languages are, of course, better fitted for close-packing than others. German, in spite of 'dichtung', is rather cumbersome. English takes up less room than French but probably the most concise is Latin. Try to put a Latin inscription into English and see how much more marble you need.

If there is a pattern, a structure to our world, there is equally a pattern or structure in the instrument we use for understanding our world – our languge. They go together. Our experience of the world modifies our language, while our language to some extent determines and fashions our understanding of the world, if not the world itself. Meaning, perception and reality are interwoven.

This chapter began with the biblical heading 'In the beginning was the word'. It ends with a matching phrase from the Indian Vedas: 'Prajapatir vai idam agre asit. Tasya vag dvitiya asit. Vag vai Paramam Brahma,' which, as I understand it, means: 'In the Beginning was God and with whom was the word. And the word was truly God.'[4] Here the Vedanta and St John's gospel appear to be in complete agreement.

Notes
1. Wilhelm von Humboldt 1767–1835, Gesammelte Werke 1841–52, quoted by E. Cassirer, *An Essay on Man,* New York, Doubleday, 1956: 134,135.
2. Max Scheler, *Wesen und Formen der Sympathie,* 1913 (Eng. edn, *The Nature of Sympathy,* Routledge, 1954).
3. M. Merleau-Ponty, *The Phenomenology of Perception,* p.182.
4. Christopher Isherwood (ed.), *Vedanta for the Western World,* London, Allen & Unwin, 1948: 150.

The Way we See

John Berger[1] tells us that artists paint women in a different way from men because they see them not as they are but as they would like them to be – dressed or undressed, in poses that flatter the artist's vanity. Femininity is always seen through male eyes and it is odd that women often seem to accept this male version of themselves. Such ways of seeing become the norm. The male is the artist or the spectator, the female the model or object of appreciation. This attitude, of course, does not stop at art; it colours the relationship between men and women everywhere. Is it, perhaps, an essential factor in the chemistry of sex, or is it no more than a habit? Is it, perhaps, reversible? I doubt it. Men and women see things too differently for each to see through the eyes of the other.

In the ancient world people used to believe that the eye was not merely a passive instrument but that rays passed from it toward the object in focus. Goethe in his *Farbenlehre* seems to have had much the same idea, suggesting that the act of seeing involved reciprocity uniting subject and object in a common bond. Just as the object affected the eye, so the eye affected the object. According to Goethe:

> The eye owes its existence to light. Out of indifferent auxiliary animal organs the light calls forth an organ for itself similar to its own nature; thus the eye is formed by the light, for the light, so that the inner light can meet the outer.

And he asks, 'Were the eye not sun-like how could we perceive light?'

The reciprocal double-take between subject and object is reflected in the phrase 'beauty lies in the eye of the beholder'. The beam from the eye of the artist alights on the subject and is reflected in the painting or sculpture from which the beam passes back to the onlooker, the art expert or aesthete. It works, too, with fashion. Fashions in women's clothes change year after year. Fashions in women's bodies change less rapidly. At one period it is considered necessary to be flat or straight as were the 'flappers' of the twenties. At another the ideal is to be busted or waisted.

In between predilection may switch from big buttocks and heavy thighs to small backsides and an athletic figure. Nowadays the preference is for wide-shouldered women.

The neck, or at least the appreciation of necks, has varied considerably over the ages. Did not the author of the *Song of Solomon* admire the monumental neck? 'Thy neck is like the tower of David builded for an armoury.' The Greeks and Romans also went in for fairly substantial necks. Then in the sixth century came the more slender column of the Byzantine neck as depicted, for instance, in the mosaics of the Holy Martyrs on the walls of Sant' Apollinare Nuovo in Ravenna. The Byzantine neck had a short-lived revival with El Greco, then much later with Modigliani and, at the present time, in fashion drawings. In Italy in the twelfth and thirteenth centuries thick necks were the fashion. Look at the women of the 'trecento' as painted by Duccio, Giotto, Simone Martini, Lorenzetti and Taddeo Gaddi. Veritable 'towers of David' nearly all of them. Then with the Pre-Raphaelites the tower of David neck was back in favour again. Rossetti was a master. Later, Picasso, too, seems to have had a liking for the formidable neck. Doesn't the way we appreciate form or try to alter nature have a deeper psychological significance?

We divide the arts into those predominantly spatial and those temporal, according to the mode of appreciation. The aesthetic appreciation of a Picasso painting, or a Raphael, or a Donatello sculpture or the West Front of Wells Cathedral is immediate and spatial, even if it takes time to absorb thoroughly. The appreciation of literature or music on the other hand is temporal and protracted since a chapter or a book cannot be read at a glance; it has to be read through. In the same way a sonata cannot be heard in a moment; it takes time for note to succeed note, phrase to follow phrase. The execution of the visual arts, however, is as time-absorbing as that of music and literature. It is only the appreciation that is different. The eye is an instrument of immediacy in space, the ear an instrument of duration in time. Light reaches us almost instantaneously – the lightning flash; sound, witness the thunder, takes time.

The way we see and hear affects the way we think and live. We like to think we are free agents, but the way we are brought up and educated to see, hear and think constrict our freedom. They colour the glasses through which we view the world. I was born and brought up in England and as a result tend to see everything through English eyes, however independent and unattached I might consider myself to be. I have a fair knowledge of French, German and Italian and have lived abroad for some years but even such literature as this knowledge opens up for me is still unavoidably coloured by my Englishness. Art and music cross frontiers more easily than literature but my knowledge and appreciation of them remains European. Science, however, and above all mathematics, knows no frontiers. Two and two make four anywhere in the world. In mathematics Englishness is of no account whatever.

Apart from mathematics and science all experience is tied to time and place, a country, a way of life, the conventions that go with it and the history behind it. Had I been born in Russia fifty years ago I would no doubt be a communist or an Orthodox believer. Had Mrs Thatcher been born in Omsk or Gorky she might have reached the Supreme Soviet and by now be fulminating against the evil West. Had Ronald Reagan been born in South Africa he would quite possibly now be arresting blacks and bombing Mozambique or Angola rather than Libya.

Such freedom as we have is restricted by time and place as the Jews under Hitler in central Europe knew to their cost. Our ideas, and outlook, likes and dislikes, are largely determined by where and when we were born and brought up. Such self-evident observations would be scarcely worth recording were it not that our rulers appear to be quite unaware of how conditioned their attitudes and outlooks are. I sometimes indulge myself with the thought that it might indeed be helpful for the peace of the world if Ronald Reagan were to live for the rest of his time in office in Soviet Russia, and for Mikhail Gorbachev to eke out his remaining days in Washington DC.

Once we recognize that our view is blinkered we can make adjustments to correct it. If we do not then we suffer from tunnel-vision – our freedom is gone and we are little more than automata, mechanisms programmed by nationality, race, colour, class, education, convention and time. Unfortunately those who govern us grow to love their blinkers.

Note
1. John Berger, *Ways of Seeing,* BBC and Penguin, 1972.

Ends and Means

It is better to play the game than to win. How old-fashioned that sounds now. If you only play to win and miss the ball then you don't play any more; you throw your racket down and abuse the referee. It is better to travel well than to arrive. This, too, sounds rather outdated. Today, arrival is all-important, and it doesn't matter how you travel or what you do to the other passengers as long as you get there. Ends determine means. As long as the ends are reached the means don't matter, except in so far as they ensure the ends. A pharmaceutical company's product has been discovered to be dangerous, or to have unacceptable side-effects. It is banned from this country. But there are other countries, preferably for the company third-world countries, where the inhabitants cannot read, or cannot read English, to which the product can be sent and where it can be marketed. So it is sent, for the ends are not so much the health of the recipients as the profits of the shareholders. Moreover the company is less likely to be sued by unsophisticated or unlettered sufferers.

This twisted ethic is, of course, an ancient one going back at least as far as Jacob and Esau, but it has been given an enormous boost by the sort of consumer-oriented society in which we live. It is widespread in politics where figures are juggled, facts mauled and statistics laundered to suit dubious ends. It infects our basic thinking. Our ideas of equality and justice are weakened because we see them as unattainable. If you can't win, it's not worth playing. If you can't get there, it's not worth setting out. Equality and justice are rarely attainable and how convenient to think one need never do anything about them. Means determine ends, for means are ends in the making.

Reason

Tout par Raison; Raison partout;
Par tout Raison.

[Everything by reason. Reason everywhere.
By every reason]

Pierre Gringoire (1475–1538)

Aristotle was one of the first and best examples of a reasoning person. To be a reasonable person, or one who holds reason in high esteem, seems to have been a mark of a civilized person down the ages. During the Age of Enlightenment reason reached its apotheosis, if that is not a contradiction in terms. Some ages have been more rational than others; there have been pendulum swings, if not fashions, in reason. Reason is clear, coherent and orderly in contrast to emotion, feeling and intuition which are, for the most part, undisciplined. But in its struggle to control the emotions reason has two major disadvantages: it is frail and it is slow, much slower than instinct or intuition. Reason is more often the servant of all our emotions. What is considered rational is often no more than the rationalization of a desire. It is the desire which provides the motive power to action for which reason merely provides the excuse. Pascal said, 'All our reasoning comes down to giving in to sentiment'. And William James[1] would appear to agree:

> Our reason is quite satisfied, in nine hundred and ninety nine cases out of every thousand of us, if it can find a few arguments that will do to recite in case our credulity is criticised by someone else. Our faith is faith in someone else's faith.

In action reason is also a lackey. Reason is the Greek tutor whose Roman master likes to have about the house and boast of but to whom he pays little attention himself. Only in the realm of mind has reason much chance of asserting itself, and that not much, beyond the groves of Academe. To Pascal there were 'two extremes; to rule out reason, and to admit nothing but reason'. Those who adhere to the former employ reason in their defence; those who stand by the latter, lack understanding. Bergson thought that intuition and reason were two different ways of attacking a problem. The reasoned way circled round it and achieved a relative knowledge; the intuitive way entered into it in an attempt to achieve absolute knowledge. But we know, from Popper if from no one else, that absolute knowledge is a chimera.

Note

1. William James, *The Will to Believe,* 1897, quoted by Margaret Knight in *William James,* Pelican, 1950: 52.

Belief and Disbelief

'Periculosum est credere et non credere.'

[It is perilous both to believe and to disbelieve.]

Jacobus Grandamicus (1588–1672)

Knowledge and understanding can be approached by two very different paths – that of reason, and that of intuition. But no one is entirely rational, nor indeed entirely intuitional. Our understanding rests on the blending and interplay of two mutually incompatible faculties. The left side of the brain is said to be the seat of reason, the right that of intuition. Nevertheless, wherever such a faculty may be situated (if that is the right word) the assumption that reason and intuition are meaningful concepts is difficult to resist.

Reason and intuition between them are seen to split humanity right down the middle. Men are seen to be more rational, women as more intuitive; men are seen as sceptics, women as believers. True or not, this is deceptive. If sceptics think it irrational to doubt what they themselves believe, what then is to distinguish them from believers? Only what they believe.[1]

Reason, too, is usually associated with clarity and hard fact, while intuition is loosely aligned with woolliness and superstition. With these are associated certain types of occupation. Scientists and engineers, for instance, are thought of as rational, whereas seamen are notoriously prone to superstition, as also are actors, acrobats and racing drivers. The horse-racing fraternity are steeped in it. Superstition seems to prevail where life is uncertain and where chance is a major factor. Security provides firm ground for reason to get a footing, but danger fosters superstition. Magic, which is allied to superstition, is according to Malinowski,[2] designed for bold and dangerous enterprises. Among the Trobriand islanders, in tasks which demanded no particular effort, no special courage of endurance, no magic was discoverable. But magic and mythology always occurred if pursuits were dangerous or uncertain.

67

The irrational approach to knowledge and understanding also embraces what has come to be known as parapsychology. A chair of parapsychology has recently been installed in the University of Edinburgh. I doubt whether it will get much support from scientists. Not many scientists consider it worthwhile to test what their training teaches them is impossible, and it is normal practice to ignore evidence which appears to conflict with accepted canons of scientific knowledge. A challenge to preconceived ideas is as unwelcome to scientists as it is to the rest of us. During the eighteenth century the French Academy of Science refused to accept evidence for the fall of meteorites, a notion which they believed to be founded on popular superstition rather than on fact. The same terror of the unknown afflicted scientists in Germany, Denmark, Switzerland, Italy and Austria, and many museums hid or threw away such exhibits as might be taken for meteorites for fear of ridicule. The professor of parapsychology at Edinburgh will need all the courage and support he can get.

Nevertheless ideas do seem to be changing. With the mechanistic science of the nineteenth century such matters as parapsychology and extra-sensory perception seemed absurdities. Now, however, the new ideas in physics seem to be pushing the door wide open for such absurdities. It will, no doubt, however, be a long time before the average scientist can bring himself to investigate, let alone accept, the paranormal. Science, after all, does not provide us with certain knowledge. As Karl Popper reminds us, every scientific statement must remain tentative for ever. Even if corroborated the corroboration is itself relative to other statements which again are tentative. There is no escape. Certain knowledge is a chimera.

Notes

1. Polanyi has claimed belief as 'the source of all knowledge'. Michael Polanyi, *Personal Knowledge,* Routledge, 1958: 266.
2. Malinowski, *The Foundations of Faith and Morals,* p.22, quoted by Cassirer, *An Essay on Man,* New Haven, 1964.

Education

Britain must surely have one of the worst-educated working populations in Western Europe. In the army, during the war, one of my duties was to censor the letters of troops writing home. I had to do the same for German prisoners. The contrast was striking. compared with the British the Germans were paragons of literature. The picture does not seem to have changed much today to judge by the popularity of the 'tabloid' press. The standard of education and technical training among workers in Britain's industries is still, we are told, not up to that of our competitors in Europe. The same, it appears, could be said of management. This seems odd in a country whose literary inheritance is second to none. Our teachers and their pupils are not more stupid than others. But it does look as if our governments have been, and still are, more than a little neglectful in this respect.

A poor education is a bad augury for the future of any country. Britain, least of all, can afford it. I am old enough to remember the First World War – the heroic but physically- and educationally-stunted Tommies, Taffies, Geordies and Jocks, compared with the great strapping lads from the dominions and the United States. What did they have that we didn't have? An attitude of mind? A less rigid class structure? A genuine democracy? A good education for all rather than for just a few? A realization that one's country meant the people, all of the people, not just the top people?

My own education was supplemented by Benn's Sixpenny Library. I still have a book on Relativity by Prof James Rice published in 1928. Then there was the Thinker's Library – those little brown books published by Watts and the Rationalist Press. They brought out H.G. Wells, John Stuart Mill, Herbert Spencer, Darwin's *Origin of Species,* Ernst Haeckel's *Riddle of the Universe,* Winwood Reade, Anatole France and a host of others. I read them avidly and became an agnostic if not quite an atheist. They were marvellous value and even if they look rather nineteenth-centuryish now I shall remain eternally indebted to them. I remember too the Tauchnitz Editions and the Insel Bücherei, all tailored to small pockets such as mine.

The universe has changed since the Thinker's Library focused its rationalist lens on it. The mechanics have gone, and with it the certainty. Heisenberg's principle of indeterminacy, and the element of irrationality perceptible in nuclear physics, have both helped to pull the carpet from under the old structure. In the Tarner Lectures at Cambridge in 1956 the Nobel physicist Erwin Schrödinger[1] claimed that the world and mind reflected each other, and that if that meant that there were as many worlds as there are minds it might be an apparent truth, but basically there was only one mind. This, he said, was the doctrine of the Upanishads. It is strange to see scientists forced by their own methodology into agreement with religion. I wonder what the old Thinker's Library would have made of it?

At the moment education in Britain is in a sorry state. Even such basic necessities as text-books are in short supply and have to be shared, while teachers are in revolt against poor pay and loss of status. Since we, as a nation, spend less on education per head of population than almost any other western nation perhaps we should not be surprised. Not only schools but universities and polytechnics are also having their grants cut. An American student is three times more likely to be able to continue with tertiary or higher education than a British one. In Japan or America over 20 per cent of the adult work force has completed a course in higher education. In Britain the figure is around 7 per cent. We score badly too against France and Germany, not only in education but in economic achievement. There seems to be a correlation here that the government has missed, for it seems intent on cutting back education still further.

In Britain there are basically two sorts of education. One for those who can afford to pay for it, and the other for those who can't. The former group comprises some 7 per cent of the population, the latter 93 per cent. The government lets the former group get on with its job but exerts greater and greater control on the latter, while its ministers send their own children, not to the schools they are so eager to control, but to those that are independent. So we have ministers, none of whom send their own children to state schools, legislating for, cutting back and controlling the education of the 93 per cent who cannot afford what they themselves can.

This is reflected in the education itself. The fortunate 7 per cent should be getting a good education in the humanities. For the remaining 93 per cent the emphasis is not so much on education as on training – a training for jobs rather than education for life. It is called education, of course, for education sounds better than training and we have no Socrates now to remind us what education really is. But in many, too many cases, it is training to fit in with non-existent job requirements, and so on. We are perpetuating, if not intensifying, a society in which the unfortunate many are being trained for the benefit of the fortunate few.

There is one respect in which education nowadays is far ahead of previous ages – the education of women. In the middle ages right up to Victorian times women's education was restricted and usually home-based. In the medieval university or 'studium generale', an exclusively male institution, the subjects studied were much the same as those a thousand years earlier, the seven liberal arts being neatly divided into the 'Trivium' and the 'Quadrivium'. The Trivium dealt with literacy – grammar, logic and rhetoric – while the Quadrivium handled numeracy – arithmetic, music, geometry and astronomy. The Quadrivium corresponded with the four Pythagorean sciences elaborated by Iamblichus and Proclus a thousand years earlier.

Nowadays we prefer a split into arts and sciences, with music which used to be considered numerate now regarded as an art rather than a science. Co-education in modern times has made comparison between the sexes possible and it appears that in general boys tend to be more numerate, girls more literate. And if we go back to the sixth century BC, we are told that Pythagoras allowed women to his lectures equally with men, but we know nothing of their predilections or achievements.

Note
1. Erwin Schrödinger, *What is Life. Mind and Matter,* Cambridge University Press, 1967: 93, 139.

History

Paul Valéry said,

> History is the most dangerous product that the chemistry of the intellect
> has ever elaborated. In the present state of the world the danger of letting
> oneself be seduced by history is greater than it ever was.

And Henry Ford said that history was bunk. About much of it he was
right, and probably the more authoritative the history the more the bunk.
In most cases the historian was not there at the time, but if he was he
would probably be too close to events to judge them impartially. If he was
not, his so-called facts are at second-hand, at third-hand, at fiftieth-hand.
Was Socrates really the man Plato and Xenophon described? Plato, it is
true, knew his mentor personally, but can one doubt that what we see is
Socrates through Plato's eyes, and probably with Plato's public in mind
also?

There is no reliable contemporary record of Christ. The authors of the
Gospels were not actual witnesses. St Mark's gospel, probably the first to
be written, is usually dated some thirty or forty years after the crucifixion.
The authors of the Gospels must have got their information from
hearsay, each of them hearing a slightly different story, or copying from
each other. It is not even certain that St Matthew's Gospel was written by
St Matthew.

Was the Trojan war as the *Iliad* described it? We cannot know. We
have no Trojan to tell us, and his version too would certainly be both
personally and nationally biased. The Second World War through British
eyes, German eyes, Russian eyes, American eyes, French eyes, Jewish eyes
or Japanese eyes is not one war but seven. Simone Weil went so far as to
say: 'Official history is believing the murderers at their word.'

Justice

British justice has often been accused of being variable according to county, to magistrate's court, to county court and so on, and with some reason. *The Times* of 18.3.1986 reprinted a letter to *The Times* of 18.3.1861 in which the writer pointed out that in many counties they do not flog criminals at all, but 'in Middlesex they flog them a good deal, in Northumberland and Staffordshire they flog them a great deal more, and in Lancashire they flog them enormously.'[1]

What, however, the writer evidently wanted to emphasize was the shocking amount of punishment given to the young children of the poor. Whereas the children of the rich never received more than 12 or 16 cuts, the poor children were flogged unmercifully. In Chester gaol a child of 8 received twenty-four lashes for 'repeated misconduct'. At Hertford a boy of 10 got sixteen lashes for stealing a piece of beef, while a man of 29 only got the same punishment for stealing twenty-nine fowls. Two 9-year olds at Faversham received fifteen lashes – one for stealing a coconut, value threepence, the other for stealing a half-pound weight, value sevenpence. Old pence. Some of the floggings were with the birch, others with the 'cat'.

The thought of magistrates condemning small children of eight and ten to be flogged with the 'cat-o-nine-tails' for minor larceny takes a bit of stomaching. True, that was over a century ago but some magistrates, even in these days, seem to regret any move towards more humane sentencing. A case in point happened some months ago: a 17-year-old girl was caught stealing a bottle of milk from a doorstep. She was sentenced to prison for twenty-one days. She had the temerity to say in her defence that she was hungry. At the present price of milk that is about one day in prison for every penny. Compared with the past where a child might have been flogged for stealing milk, or even hanged for stealing a sheep, there is obviously some improvement, but it appears to have little to do with justice. The rectitude of the magistrates in question must take some living up to. I wonder how they manage to live up to it themselves. Has none of them, ever, got off a bus without paying, or perhaps tried to diddle the income tax for a bit more than the price of a bottle of milk?

The inappropriateness of a prison sentence for such a trivial aberration should surely be evident even to such magistrates when our gaols are overflowing, with often three to a cell and God knows how many to a latrine bucket. We have more people in prison per head of population than almost any western country. It is true we are beaten in this unenviable league table by Turkey, South Africa and the Soviet Union, but who wants to rival them? Are our people more 'wicked', or our magistrates and judiciary more punitive? I find it difficult to believe that the British are so much more wicked than the French, Germans or the Dutch.

To send people convicted of violence to prison is no doubt necessary, but why do we also send petty thieves, inadequates, drunks, prostitutes, pregnant women, the mentally defective, and those unconvicted? We must love sending people to prison. With the number of prison inmates topping 48,000 and, if things do not change for the better, continuing to rise, the only answer apparently acceptable to the government is not to review sentencing procedure but to build more and more prisons. The Red Queen in *Alice in Wonderland* could hardly do better: 'Off with their heads!'

What kind of people, one wonders, would want to become magistrates? Those who like power? Those so convinced of their own rectitude that they consider themselves fitted to judge others? Those who need some letters after their names? Those who like the idea of punishment? Or those who so love justice that they are prepared to sacrifice time and money for it? Let us hope the latter. A magistrate, like a juror, should be reluctant to become one. As for judges, why do they have to sit in monstrous wigs and flowing robes? Is it to inflate their egos, or to cow the rest of us? Would not justice be better served if they were to sit in their ordinary clothes? The flummery of tradition is one thing and no doubt has its place in the theatre, in processions, in masques and in fancy-dress balls, but what has it to do with justice?

Criminal justice and social justice are related, for social injustice leads to crime. Social injustice is often the material cause of many kinds of crime. Hunger in a society in which others are well-fed is a form of social injustice. If the girl mentioned above had not been hungry it is unlikely that she would have taken the milk. Similarly, opulence in a society in which most people are poor is a sign of social injustice. It is not necessary to believe in equality for all to believe that a greater measure of social justice than we have is not only desirable but also possible. Social injustice is often the result of greed, and is therefore ingrained pretty deeply.

At home we are no doubt used to the excesses of millionaires, pop stars and the flamboyant buccaneers of the money market, but it is not often we get a glimpse of what goes on behind the scenes in the home life of a ruler. The Filipinos have been vouchsafed such a glimpse with the flight of their erstwhile president Marcos and family. An ornate bathroom, with jacuzzi and a 24-carat-gold basin, may not sound out of the way in a palace, but the sight of sixty-seven racks of dresses for Imelda Marcos, more than a thousands gowns, nearly 3,000 pairs of shoes, 500 bras, 200 boxes of unopened stockings, another 200 boxes of girdles, together with a store-room stacked with boxes of television sets, video recorders and computers must take a lot of getting used to. This would surely seem a little excessive in a country like America, but in a nation with a population of 55 million, trying to struggle out of grinding poverty it is not just bizarre, it is obscene.

A little less bizarre but almost as obscene in a country with millions on or below the poverty line was a report in *The Times*. It said that several directors of companies in Britain were nearing the million pounds a year mark in directors' fees. This would be understandable if the workers who made this bonanza possible were also munificently paid. Generally our workers are among the lowest paid in western Europe while being constantly exhorted to keep wages down.

Without social justice, justice itself becomes twisted. In monarchic, aristocratic, oligarchic or dictatorial states there has often been an enormous discrepancy between what the rich allow the poor to own. And in democracies? Well, to take our own as an example, the top 1 per cent own 50 per cent of the shares and nearly 50 per cent of the land; the top 10 per cent own 90 per cent of the shares and about 80 per cent of the land. The young Duke of Westminster owns some 138,000 acres including large sections of the West End of London. A tiny proportion of the population, about 5 per cent go to public schools (i.e. private schools) but this 5 per cent accounts for 47 per cent of members of parliament, 60 per cent of permanent secretaries, 81 per cent of principal judges, 86 per cent of army officers and 85 per cent of Anglican bishops. The figures are for 1981 and during the succeeding years the numbers attending private schools have gone up 1 or 2 per cent. While privatization has resulted in many more share-owners, many shares have already been sold and bought back by big institutions. The situation is manifestly inequitable and one might ask why, in a democracy, the vast majority do not seek to correct it. The answer is that most are unaware of the enormity of such discrepancies and, moreover, our rulers are adept at getting the general public to accept the situation as natural, inevitable and even just.

To some extent, of course, the situation is inevitable. Complete equality is a chimera, and no one in his right mind expects it. But the degree of difference is what is disturbing and also demeaning. As with a liquid solution every social solution has a top and a bottom, whether right-wing or left-wing, capitalist or communist, hierarchical or egalitarian. Nor matter which political system, in the end the bottom is made up of the same people – those deprived of money, property, privilege, health, and so on. A revolution such as the Russian revolution merely turns the solution upside down. When all the particles have settled once more it will be found that the same people are still at the bottom.

It is nevertheless possible for the individual, if clever enough or ambitious enough or ruthless enough, to rise to the top without too much disturbance of the layers, but not the mass. If one wants to get on in this world it is advisable, if not essential, to side with the right people – capitalists in capitalist countries, socialists in socialist countries – unless it is evident that a revolution is coming to the boil, or a military coup in the offing, which has every likelihood of succeeding. Then a change of sides, provided it is well-timed, may prove advantageous.

The self-interested individual on his way up corrects no injustice. Instead, he confirms it. Only a well-informed, well-disciplined, well-intentioned people can radically re-adjust the balance. When, however, they are fed by the system on tabloid mis-information, false values and wishful thinking, it will no doubt be some time before social inequity is replaced by social justice.

Note

1. Over the years the severest 'justice' has often been inflicted on those least able to stand up for themselves. Under Henry VIII vagabonds were tied to a cart-tail and whipped. On being arrested a second time the whipping was repeated and half an ear sliced off. On the third arrest vagabonds were executed as hardened criminals.

   Under James I beggars were publicly whipped or imprisoned. Repeated offenders were branded with an 'R' on the left shoulder and set to hard labour. If they were then caught begging again they were executed without mercy.

   Many such, labelled 'vagabonds', had been driven to beggary by forcible expropriation from the soil. (See Marx, *Capital,* Chap. XXVII.)

Double Standards

Recently a number of people have been charged with defrauding the Department of Health and Social Security by claiming more from the state than they were entitled to. The defrauders were denounced and execrated in the press. The government instituted an army of investigators to spy on the public, while the police staged an elaborate trick to catch the miscreants. They succeeded in netting numbers of innocent people who, when brought to court, were immediately acquitted.

Still more recently the City of London has come under censure for fraudulent dealing involving hundreds of millions of pounds, implicating not only merchant banks but the Bank of England itself. In this case the treatment by press, government, police and public was rather different. The first reaction was denial, and the person responsible for bringing the accusation was denounced and derided. Later, as evidence became substantiated the prevailing attitude seemed to be 'well, there are always a few rotten apples but on the whole the City can be trusted to police itself'. The police squad brought in to clean up the matter was of a size and training quite inadequate to deal with the situation. The government, realizing that this could be political dynamite on account of their supporters' involvement, hastened to bring in a bill to allay criticism and clean up the affair. The City was left to continue to police its own transactions.

Apparently while the government considered it essential to come down hard on petty thievery, the big boys could be left largely to the supervision of people of their own kind. The moral seems to be, if you want to get away with it don't settle for five pounds because the state will come down on you like a ton of bricks. Settle instead for half a million, implicate the City of London and the Bank of England, and with luck no one will touch you.

Why is it that such double standards are not recognized for what they are? It appears that people are rarely inclined to attack those above them in the social scale, but are only too ready to criticize those they consider to be beneath them. In hen runs there is a recognized pecking order. It operates always from the top downwards. The stronger attack the weaker. In hierarchical class systems the same law seems to operate. The better off attack the worse off, while the worse off attack those even worse off than themselves. Hence everyone abhors the scrounger of a few pounds, while the city rogue operator, or crook who gets away with millions, is often more an object of envy than of contempt. We would all like to be rich, judging by the appeal of soap operas like *Dallas,* but just getting enough to pay the gas bill has little romantic appeal.

Another instance of the pecking order in operation is shown in that there are few people so hard on the working class as those who have just risen out of it, and similarly those who have just left lower-middle for upper-middle. Many, it seems, cannot scale the class wall without treading others down. The qualities required of a good class-climber are not those of tolerance, sympathy and comradeship. They are more often ruthlessness, arrogance towards one's peers, and obsequiousness towards one's superiors. This does not mean that no one can rise out of his class without such qualities. Many have done it, but with greater difficulty.

A government of aristocrats is more likely to be benevolent to the poor than a government of ambitious go-getters. The former may well have the vestige of *noblesse oblige.* It has been at the game much longer, has got what it wants, and can afford to sit back. But the latter is still in the process of consolidating its position, and sees still more to be won. And since it can't demand it from the rich without endangering its position, it is inevitably the poor that suffer. There are double standards here again. Those coming up in the world are admired; those pushed out and finding it difficult to cope have no public sympathy.

We are told by the nabobs of big business, the Confederation of British Industry, that wages are too high, that a 6.25 per cent increase for employees in manufacturing industry is too much. In a table of pay increases for 1983, published in the *Sunday Times,* the increases of Britain's 100 top company directors averaged 28.3 per cent. When people getting a 28 per cent increase accuse others getting 6 per cent of having too much we are surely entitled to ask just what is happening and to question the way in which business is conducted. When employees see that employers, on top of colossal salaries, are getting a further increase of four and a half times their own (i.e. four and a half times in percentage terms which could mean thirty times more in actual cash) they are scarcely likely to work for less, or believe a word their employers say. In a free and fair society differences in income could be accommodated without envy or resentment. But when the aims of society are patently to get more and more of everything, regardless of those getting less and less, then differences in income become of paramount importance. Those who are greedy cannot, in honour, preach abstinence for others.

Greed and envy are no doubt part of human nature, but they are fed and over-fed in a consumer society by the press, advertising and television. One can hardly hear a broadcast on a golf championship, or tennis at Wimbledon, or snooker, or boxing, without the announcer saying how many thousands of pounds the winner has pocketed, as if this were the main purpose of the exercise. As indeed it is rapidly becoming. In South Africa, I read, one cricketer is being paid 100 Rand (about £30) for every four runs he scores, a bonus of 500 Rand for every half century and 1000 Rand a century. Two centuries will net him 5,000 Rand and a catch 150 Rand. Strangely enough this is still called sport, not business.

Authority

Systems of government may be either hierarchical, or egalitarian. Hierarchical systems are monarchies, oligarchies, plutocracies, aristocracies, dictatorships or juntas. Egalitarian systems are – well, on second thoughts, it is difficult to name any. Democracies may make claim to an attempt at egalitarianism but, in practice, do not attempt too much. Usually they are not democracies but oligarchies pretending to be democracies. I suppose it is debatable whether a true democracy is possible. In his essay on 'Power' Bertrand Russell says that in Sicily during the war with Carthage the rich favoured oligarchy and the poor democracy. But when supporters of democracy got the upper hand their leader usually became a tyrant.

What are governments for? Marx pointed out that one reason for a state's existence was to ensure the continuance of privilege to the ruling class. In a feudal state this meant keeping the landed nobility in power. In a capitalist state it means keeping the moneyed classes and the bourgeoisie in power. In a hierarchical system of state socialism (and regrettably this means most socialist states) it means protecting the ruling bureaucracy with all the privileges it has arrogated to itself. In totalitarian states, whether of right or left, voting is little more than a farce. Even in so-called democracies, if the people's education has been neglected, the ballot is not much more than a cunning swindle which benefits largely the powerful and privileged.

According to Joseph Pierre Proudhon[1] to be governed is to be watched over, inspected, spied on, directed, legislated, regimented, closed in, indoctrinated, preached at, controlled, assessed, evaluated, censored and commanded by those who have neither the right, nor the wisdom, nor the virtue to do so. We all know the sort of government Proudhon means. We still have many of them throughout the world and our own is not entirely guiltless. Less government is usually better than more government. But what if one is not governed? Anarchy may be an ideal state but it requires an impossibly high standard of moral integrity from all if it is not to degenerate to the level of the government it has replaced, or worse.

The *Tao-teh-Ching* recommends: 'The state should be governed as we cook small fish, without much business.' And Mencius remarked: 'The people are of supreme importance; the altars to the gods of earth and grain come next; last comes the ruler.' It is difficult to imagine any present-day government subscribing to any such advice.

This century, surely, has witnessed the apotheosis of everything Proudhon despised in government? The Nazi government was supremely authoritarian, so still is the Soviet government, and so are all those totalitarian regimes from communist China to fascist Chile. Our own government, though not quite in the same league, has also been accused of authoritarianism. Indeed it certainly could be said to be more authoritarian than its predecessors. It could also be said that government without some authority is an impossibility.

But there are degrees in this as in everything else. According to Erich Fromm we accept authority as an escape from freedom. Freedom of choice is a burden. 'We don't know enough; we don't want the bother of finding out: let someone else decide for us.' This fits in perfectly with the desire of another to dominate. The authoritarian is fascinated by power while at the same time having contempt for the powerless. Even the sight of a powerless person is enough to prompt an attack or humiliation. With this element of sado-masochism there is a mutual link between dominance and submission. At the level of government, the more authoritarian the rulers, the more acquiescent or self-abasing the ruled. This could perhaps explain much of electoral apathy. Many people seem to prefer to be ordered about than to think for themselves – a gratuitous gift to governments, even so-called democratic ones. A people that voluntarily gags and binds itself, often through fear of upsetting convention, makes light work for the ambitious and power hungry.

In totalitarian states, whether of right or left, the people can only be told what the government thinks is good for them. Secrecy is all important. In democratic states the people have a right to know what the government is doing in their name. In the United States this right is generally respected. They have 'open government'. So it is, in more or less degree, with many other democratic states. The British government, however, does not in general like the people to know. Freedoms are to be defended, but the freedom of information, apparently, is not one of them. The Official Secrets Act, for instance, is often applied whenever the government does not want something to be known. It can, and does, claim that the Act is applicable even when the subject has not a remote connection with national defence for which, specifically, the act was originally instituted.

This authoritarian grip of government over people is further strengthened by technology, and especially by information technology. We are told we are now moving from an industrial society into an information society, from consumer goods to consumer communication, from things themselves to facts about things. The western world is inundated with radio and television, with telexes, cordless telephones, car telephones, scanners, word-processors, computers and information systems of all kinds. The police have computer banks containing God knows what data on probably most of us. The policeman on the beat can ring up and get information on any one of us within minutes.

Industry has its own information banks, so does insurance, the banking system and the stock exchange. Private data-bank companies can buy information about anyone from councils selling electoral rolls. It will cost them about a penny per person and they then sell it again to detective agencies, or literally anyone, for a pound – a very handsome profit indeed. There seems to be no supervision to protect the public and no check on accuracy, though the new Data Protection Act may give some limited protection. Government computer records may be available to the police and, for all one knows, may soon be available to insurance, banks and commercial firms. On the new central index of the Department of Health and Social Security absolutely everyone will be included.

Many people have already lost jobs through inaccurate data-bank information; information which they were totally ignorant of, cannot correct and which probably will remain with them for ever. There is now, we learn, a new type of machine for reading and computerizing the information on passports. One will soon not be able to leave the country on holiday, or be allowed back, without some machine going through one's life history first and giving its permission.

The amount of information stored must be colossal, but how accurate is it? For, of course, the mandarins behind such a system with the 'facts' can question us, but we can get nothing out of them. We, an information society, are denied the information. George Orwell must be turning in his grave. Everyone is tabbed, typed, docketed, numbered with such information as home address, workplace, car number, income, liabilities, married status, unmarried status, court record, prison record, debts, political affiliation, political activity, religion, class, social standing, trades-union affiliation, profession, race, colour, and much else besides. A totalitarian state could hardly wish for more. Do we protest? Do we demand safe-guards? Do we demand to know? Hardly. We still have a choice, but for how much longer? Every new such technique weakens the power of the people and strengthens the power of the authorities.

Note

1. Proudhon (1809–65) considered property, like slavery, to be the murder of individual freedom. To him property was theft, (la propriété c'est le vol). His ideal was perfect freedom, equality and justice, that all labour, mental and physical, should be remunerated at the same scale and that government was an evil. *Qu'est-ce que la Propriété?*, 1840 and *Systeme des Contradictions Economiques ou Philosophie de la Misere*, 1846.

Law and Order

In public life the maintenance of law and order is the prerogative of the police. In recent years law and order has been less noticeable, but the presence of the police more so. In the 1930s the police were regarded as servants of the people. The constable on the beat wore no collar and tie, nor did he have radio communication with the local police station. He was known to those living on his beat, and he knew them. Now that the police are less servants of the public they wear collars and ties, and constables, or 'bobbies' as they used to be called, now prefer to be called officers. They do not know the public as they used. Fast cars and technology, coupled with a feeling of power, come between them and those they are supposed to serve. At times they appear to become even enemies of the people. The police have been given more power and the public have less – a step, even if a small one, towards an authoritarian state.

These days the police seem to be rarely out of the papers, and often it has little to do with the enormous increase in crime. Britain, which used to be the envy of other nations for its law and order, is now probably the most crime-ridden country in Europe. To cap it all, the police have been accused, not always without reason, of racism, brutality and corruption. At one time the police were seen but rarely heard. They got on with the job quietly and, on the whole, pretty efficiently. Now hardly a week goes by without some chief constable pontificating in the daily press or on the radio. Our streets are deafening with the whine of police sirens.

Our erstwhile much admired 'friendly bobby' seems to have metamorphosed into something quite other, if not as yet an aggressive bully, at least a rather doubtful friend of the people. This is not an entirely new departure, however, for even fifty years ago, while he was regarded as a friend in middle- and upper-class areas, in poor districts he was often the enemy. He was seen as protector of the landlords rather than the tenants, of the exploiters rather than of those exploited. As one who worked for several years in a poor district of east London, but who lived in a middle-class area, I found the different attitudes of police to people and of people to police quite striking. Where I lived they were friends. Where I worked they were enemies. There were no evictions where I lived. They were of almost daily occurrence where I worked.

Perhaps there is no way out of this. Authority is always on the side of those who have power; those who have power are those who have money. This dichotomy is even carried through into parliament. Relationships between the police and the Conservatives are cordial, on the whole, for Conservatives are the 'haves'. With Labour, the party of the 'have nots', the relationship is much less easy.

A disturbing fact about the public's relationship with the police is that there is often no redress for a private citizen who suffers from police error, neglect or violence. There is a complaints authority to which we may take our cases but since it, too, is run by the police the chances of an unbiased hearing are poor. The impression left in the mind of the injured party is that it is impossible to win, while the police can get away with anything. The obvious, and just, remedy would be to take complaints out of police hands and assign them to an independent body. This the police vigorously oppose, but it is difficult to see why any democratic government should not do just that. The fact that the Home Office still side-steps the issue is worrying. It does suggest it might be hankering a little after totalitarian control.

Law and order are essential if a society is to have any permanence. Indeed law and order should be the natural outcome of any fair and just society, not imposed from above. As it is law and order have to be balanced against the claims of individual and collective freedoms. In fact, those countries in which law and order are most in evidence are in general not democracies but totalitarian states, either right or left. An obsession with law and order on the part of a government means restriction of freedom on the part of the people.

Moreover, little attention appears to be paid to the causes of lawlessness and disorder. When violence and unrest are on the increase as at present, the government's response is to clamour for more law and order. Police powers are increased, and the police are armed with riot shields, tear gas and plastic bullets. It does not seem to occur to the Home Office that this is clamping down the lid on a boiling cauldron instead of turning down the gas. It may be dealing with symptoms but it is doing very little positive about causes.

The causes are, of course, multifarious. But among them must surely be poverty in the inner-city areas with its frustration, unemployment, homelessness, racial discrimination, lack of prospects and realization of being at the bottom of the pile in a society whose main aim appears to be the accumulation of money, and material goods. And, of course, there's a measure of pure bloody-mindedness.

It is noteworthy that violence tends to occur in just those areas where poverty, unemployment and disillusion are rife, not in the well-heeled suburbs. Houses are falling into disrepair for lack of money; few new houses are being built; social services have declined and subsidies have been cut. All this is fuel to the fire and month by month the government continues to add to it. But since the fuel is of the government's own making it cannot admit to any connection between the fuel and the fire it feeds. How much easier to clamp down the lid and ascribe it all to 'wickedness'.

It would be foolish to deny that wickedness may play a part in it; obviously it does. But the energy which manifests in violence in a deprived area might well be turned to more productive ends if the environment and conditions were more favourable. It seems more than probable that destructiveness in people is proportional to the restriction of legitimate outlets, whether real or felt. Erich Fromm describes destructiveness as the outcome of unlived life. The brutal murderer may well be a decorated hero in a war, but in peace his aptitude for violence is out of place. He may be the same man, but the conditions are utterly different. Many of us are not criminals largely because we do not need to break the law. The law is on our side, not against us; the environment is on our side; the conventions are on our side. When we have so much going for us it would be mad to break out of the charmed circle. If we do it is usually into some respectable crime such as fraud in the City, with no need for physical violence.

The answer to disruption in society must surely be to investigate the causes and deal with them. The difficulty is that this would involve a more democratic, less hierarchical approach, and governments, of whatever colour, while democratic in theory tend to be hierarchical in action. We would have to do some radical re-thinking towards changing to a society in which imposed law and order, as well as unrest and violence, are minimal. This would mean starting from the bottom up as the initiative would have to come from the people. No authority willingly initiates its own dissolution. The process of change would have to be gradual, here and there, with small groups working together, exchanging knowledge and expertise. Good instincts would be revived. Self-help, co-operation and mutual aid could alleviate and improve the condition of those most in need. The aim should be for a steady, gradual movement which, in the long term, could transform society radically but non-violently.

With the causes tackled, the symptoms should have little to feed on. Gradually, step by step, we might find ourselves in a society where order is on the side of liberty, and law helping those most in need of it. If this sounds like an unattainable Utopia we need not lose too much sleep over it. We have to have aims, and often the more unobtainable the better. It is the direction and the effort which matter.

Untouchables

Are we creating a class of untouchables? In 1987 a group of people was driven from Salisbury Plain to Savernake Forest, from lay-by to disused aerodrome, not only by a large force of police but also by the concentrated venom of the gutter press. They were described as dirty, feckless, shiftless unemployables living on the state.

The description was right in one respect: they were unemployable, for there were over three million unemployed, even after the government's repeated ploys to cut the figure by adjusting the method of counting. These people were seen as committing the unforgiveable sin of opting out of this society which they saw as greedy, ruthless, money-grabbing and mean.

They were not as spotlessly clean as their denigrators, partly because hot baths are difficult without facilities and one cannot very well take a tub in the middle of a field surrounded by scores of police. The tabloid press painted the so-called 'hippies' in the worst light possible, playing on the lowest octave in the gamut of human or inhuman emotion. Members of Parliament raged and demanded draconian laws to further corral and harass a disturbing but essentially harmless group of people. Even the Home Secretary likened them to 'medieval brigands', conveniently forgetting that his party supported an aristocracy descended in great part from real medieval brigands, not harmless drop-outs.

We like to believe that to be British is to be free, but it appears that freedom is of a rather fragmentary nature. We can have freedom to go where we want 'without let or hindrance' as our passport indicates, but we are not so free to opt out, to go against convention. We welcome dissidents in countries beyond the iron curtain, but dissidents in our own country are not at all welcome. The bureaucrats, and the gutter press, by whipping up public sentiment, are conspiring, albeit unwittingly, to manufacture a class of untouchables. It is, of course, much easier to deal with them once firmly labelled as such. Hitler sent his gypsies to concentration camps because he could not stand dissidents either. We, if we are to have any self-respect, must find other means.

We cannot go on harrowing people in this way. It is not necessary to have them on our doorstep or in our back garden, which they would reject anyway, but some way must be found for providing them with a resting place and reasonable facilities. The army has been given large tracts of Salisbury plain to play with and destroy. Surely it should be possible to find a small portion of land on which our own dissidents could find asylum. If not we shall stand in sore need of another Mahatma Gandhi.

There is an ancient Sanskrit formula 'tat tvam asi' (thou art that) which means to see oneself in others. Instead of which we objectify others. We see them not so much as people like us but more as objects for our manipulation or as obstacles to our own objectives. Gandhi saw beyond this to the people themselves. Martin Buber in his book *I and Thou* differentiates between the relationship 'I and Thou' and 'I and It'. We live in a culture in which 'I and It' is all important and 'I and Thou' almost forgotten. Once again we must say with Schumacher that it is people that matter. Otherwise we may soon be regarding the unemployed as untouchables as well.

Terms of Reference

To the sceptical onlooker it appears that when a government decides to go down a certain path and something goes wrong its first reaction is to deny it. Then when the denial is seen as unsupportable and an inquiry is demanded, the inquiry is refused; if not refused, at least delayed, no doubt in the hope that if put off long enough it will lose publicity value and be forgotten. If protest, however, continues and the prolonged delay begins to look suspicious, the next move is to limit the investigation to some less-damaging aspect of the matter, and what is known as 'Terms of Reference' are established.

Lawyers are brought in to draft the framework of the inquiry to exclude, as far as possible, anything which might reflect adversely on the government's actions or miscalculations. Any matters outside the framework are deemed to be beyond the terms of reference and therefore not subject to judgment. With all criticism concentrated on that aspect least damaging to the government the question is rarely asked whether the path chosen should be a matter of inquiry. The path chosen is accepted to be the correct one, indeed assumed in the terms of reference to be correct. 'Something went wrong down there. That is all you need to know.' The question whether down there was the right way to go in the first place has become irrelevant and is beyond the terms of reference. The idea of re-thinking the whole matter from scratch and perhaps choosing another direction is anathema.

As a case in point we are saddled with nuclear power. It is assumed that we will not be able to maintain our standard of living without it, though estimates of our needs are contradictory and little money has been spent on developing alternatives. Regardless of how many incidents, leaks or explosions may occur the government is determined to go on with it – until perhaps there is an explosion in its own backyard. Probably it will need precisely that before it can be persuaded to think again.

Freedom and Oppression

Attempts to free peoples from oppression are often short-lived. Bertrand Russell once described the history of the French revolution as – fanaticism, victory, despotism, collapse and reaction. It was indeed short-lived. Can we apply the same formula to the Russian revolution? Fanaticism, victory, despotism . . . It has stuck there, for the last seventy years. But then Russia has known little but despotism in all its history. It looks as though the blood of the Tsars and the Boyars still flows in the veins of the rulers of modern Russia.

Will the Russian people ever be allowed their own freedom? And what would they do with it if they had it? For the great majority have never known freedom. The autocracy and bureaucracy of the Tsars has been replaced by the autocracy and bureaucracy of Lenin, then Stalin and their kind, and shows little sign of 'withering away'. 'Proletarians of all nations unite! You have nothing to lose but your chains.' But they still have their chains in many countries, and few harsher and more rigid than those forged in the USSR. The revolution with the best of motives, to free the common people from oppression, has metamorphosed into an iron-handed, autocratic bureaucracy, conservative, secretive and puritanical; yet so orthodox and establishment-minded as to excite the envy of any would-be dictator with fascist leanings anywhere. The last word that could be applied to it now is 'revolutionary'.

Many so-called democratic governments must regard with envy the constraint on unions, the outlawing of strikes, the strength of the militia, the control of the press, the prohibition of popular demonstration against government action, and the total absence of any opposition party. As democrats they dare not openly admit to such feelings. Nevertheless they try, step by step, to introduce legislation against trade unions, strikes and demonstrations; meanwhile increasing the power of the police. Authoritarianism is a highly-infectious disease.

But now, just when the authoritarianism and secrecy of our own government is increasing, the iron hold of Mikhail Gorbachev's Russia on

91

its people is beginning to loosen. 'Glasnost', or 'openness' is the word now in favour. How far this new freedom will go no one can say, and many in the 'old guard' of conservative bureaucrats will oppose it, but at least it is a step in the right direction. Dissidents have been freed and critical discussion permitted in press and on television. A small step, perhaps, and a long way to go if the Russians are to have the sort of freedom to which western countries have been used. It's a step to be warmly welcomed, nevertheless. It will be a pity if this new bid for freedom in the Soviet Union has to be balanced by an increasing desire for authoritarianism in our own country.

Apartheid • Apart-Hate • Separate Development

I do not like to recall that I was once a supporter of apartheid, though I did not see it as such at the time. In the early 1930s I lived in the highlands of Kenya when relations between whites and blacks were friendly. It was some years before the eruption of Mau Mau.

The bungalow was built of mud and wattle with a thatched roof. There was, of course, no water, gas or electricity laid on, nor radio. Lighting was by kerosene lamps. Water had to be brought from the river Nzoia and boiled. Milk from the native cows had to be boiled also. We ate buck and guinea fowl and occasionally 'samaki' – fish from lake Victoria Nyanza. To have a shower, a kerosene can full of water was poured over one, standing in a tub. Life was primitive. At an altitude of some 6,000 feet and only forty miles from the equator it was rarely too hot, and never too cold. It was a dry heat, and one could see fifty miles or more without difficulty, the air was so sharp and clear.

We had a cook, two or three other servants to wait in the bungalow, and gangs of workers on the estate which grew maize and coffee. The workers came from neighbouring tribes, with a few Luo and Nandi from farther afield. The Nandi usually brought their spears and clubs to work, though not in any threatening way; it was their custom. They took them everywhere. Like the Masai, whom they physically resembled, they were pastoral nomads and looked after the cattle. We whites never carried arms.

Our form of apartheid was not unfriendly, but the *watu*, the men, were kept in their place. Every worker had to have a pass-book to be shown on demand. The *watu* could not speak English and we spoke a kind of kitchen Ki-Swahili which they seemed to understand. The settlers had bought up and annexed most of the best land while the Africans lived in their reserves. Since the settlers needed a labour force a 'hut tax' was imposed and the only way for an African to pay this was to work on white land. To earn enough to pay the tax the workers had to leave their reserves and live as temporary squatters on white land for part of the year. Then they returned to their families in the reserve.

93

At the time I saw nothing wrong with this. I had been educated to see nothing wrong with it. My generation had grown up in the all-pervading ethos of Empire, an ethos which few had dared to question. The fact that the Africans rarely seemed to question it helped us in maintaining both our position and our illusion. They did not seem to realize how they had been despoiled of their own land and demeaned to become hewers of wood and drawers of water to an alien race. They cheerfully embraced us, their exploiters, as friends. Later, when they had a chance to educate themselves, they saw how they had been tricked and wanted their land back. Now, years later, they have got it, at least in name, but I fear they have been tricked again, this time by their own people.

Apartheid is a disease not confined to South Africa. It infects every oligarchy, every privileged community anywhere. In Britain, even to this day, there is still an apartheid between the accents of public school/Oxbridge and the rest of the nation. It is less than it was, but it is still there. There is an apartheid between the 'haves' and the 'have nots'. There is still apartheid between those 'out of the top drawer' and those not so well-placed. The Prime Minister, who has herself moved up a drawer or two, has done something to ameliorate this particular divide, but has aggravated others, especially those of race and colour.

It is rare in the inner-city slums to come across prosperous middle-class people. The well-off do not want to know how the other half lives. The inner cities vote Labour, while middle-class suburbs and the prosperous shires of the south-east vote Conservative. It is not so much freedom of choice, but a vote depending on income and privilege.

This is supposed to be a free and democratic society. In theory the Ritz is open to everyone, but in practice you need to have money. The law is open to everyone, but in practice you can't get very far without money. Medical treatment is open to everyone, but in practice you may have to wait years for an operation unless you can pay for private treatment. Men and women are equal, but in practice women have a struggle to be treated as equal. White and black are equal before the law; but in practice?

In theory we have a democratic society, but in practice it is oligarchic. Education could hardly be more oligarchic with its cheque-book apartheid. There is not even the pretence of justice or evenhandedness. The wealthy send their offspring to private schools to be taught by the best of the teaching profession. The rest, something like 95 per cent, have to fall back on the state which is as grudging as it can get away with. Such apartheid naturally perpetuates the retention of privilege by the few at the expense of the many. The class war goes on. And the underprivileged are accused of starting it, not those who have been quietly waging it for generations.

In a free and fair society access to a good education should be the right of all and not be determined by the ability to pay. Schools should be open to all who wish to take advantage of them regardless of money, class, race, colour or religion, and there should be variety, which the state should foster. There should be freedom for teachers to start up their own schools, even experimental schools, provided they can establish their fitness.

Apartheid has a long history. The Greeks described non-Greeks as 'Barbaroi', barbarians. The Romans described those neither Greek nor Roman as barbarians, while the Greeks still regarded the Romans as barbaric. Hitler's Germany, had it won the war, would have turned Russians and those of 'inferior stock' into servants or serfs in the service of the master race.

Work • Capitalism • Communism

Wealth is like muck. It is not good but if it be spread.
Francis Bacon

Why do we have millions of people out of work? Why is there anyone unemployed? Surely there is more than enough work for everyone to last a life-time. What prevents people who want to work from working? One reason could be that work is limited because of the peculiar way in which we have arranged things. It is limited to suit employers, the market and profit. The value of people is not in themselves but in how much they can produce and for how little. When the market says they produce too little for too much they are put on the dole and paid a pittance to do nothing.

The system is not only mad, it is degrading and soul-destroying. Then why do we stand for it? Because the system suits those in control – the employers and the market – and their influence is paramount. Moreover we have got used to it. Hasn't it always been there? It seems normal and we don't question it because we don't like the abnormal. Any alternative is always pictured as far worse, and not only by those who profit from the system. Any connection between the system and unemployment is carefully ignored or vigorously denied. We are told the cause of unemployment is the unemployed: they won't work for the money that the market insists they are worth. For the system, human beings do not exist. They are cyphers, items in statistics. Like wine lakes and sugar mountains they are a glut on the market. E.F. Schumacher's economics were an 'economics as if people mattered'.[1] Obviously people do not matter very much in our system. What is to be done? – change the system or go on sacrificing the people? The answer is plain: sacrifice the people.

The system referred to is obviously capitalism. Would communism or any other -ism be any better? As an ideal, possibly. But in practice? It is the practice, not the ideal, that materially affects us. Capitalism goes back a long way; how far it's difficult to say. Some put its origin in the sixteenth century, some in the previous century, and some later. Lewis Mumford puts it sometime in the thirteenth century, and claims that in its later form capitalism turned five of the deadly sins, including envy and greed, into virtues since they were seen as incentives to business. Compared with communism, however, capitalism is a newcomer. Communism was mandatory for Plato's 'guardians' in *The Republic*. The early Christian church, following the instructions of its founder, practised a form of communism as did the monasteries later. In the middle ages many religious orders both taught and practised it. Thomas More's *Utopia* was a communist state.

Nowadays when we speak of communism we call it Marxist communism, but when we talk of capitalism we mean nineteenth-century or twentieth-century capitalism. Both words have had so much mud thrown at them that in communist countries capitalism is a dirty word, while in capitalist countries communism is an even dirtier word. Whereas capitalism is a tangible reality, communism is, at best, only partial. The actuality, at least in the USSR, is a sort of totalitarian state-capitalism which the Russians call socialist and the rest of us call communist.

In the communism espoused by Marx the state should have withered away. Instead the opposite has happened; the state is all-powerful. But the West is not going to drop the word communism because of that. It is far too useful a smear word. Call someone a commie and there is no need for further argument; he is damned. Similarly it is only necessary to call someone a bloated capitalist, or a fascist hyena, for all reasonable discussion to crumble. If it weren't for smear words we would all have to think a bit more, which is often uncomfortable.

Capitalism means the acquisition of capital by individuals which enables them to increase their material wealth through private enterprise. Communism means the sharing of things in common. Capitalism is, therefore, divisive, self-seeking and individualistic; communism unitive egalitarian and altruistic. While this description of capitalism is no doubt recognizable that of communism is not. The ideal and practice of capitalism do bear some relationship to each other. In communism, the ideal and practice are so divorced as to offer little hope of re-union.

Capitalism first embraced, then replaced, usury. In England usury was prohibited as far back as 1197. It had been condemned by Aristotle, and later forbidden by the Church. In the sixteenth century, theologians of the University of Paris fulminated against the opening of state banks, claiming that usury was a sin against Christianity. Later, opinions began to change. Usury was allowed to non-Christians, since their faith would not be thus compromised. In the nineteenth century that prophet of Utilitarianism, Jeremy Bentham, came out in its favour with the publication of his *Defence of Usury*. It soon became the money-lender's bible. Nowadays we don't use the word usury any more. Capitalism has taken it over in more senses than one. Even the Church does not seem greatly concerned. Money and 'the market' are the altars at which we now worship.

In modern life, economics is geared not so much to provide everyone with the necessities of life as to make a profit regardless of whether or not necessities are provided. The anthropologist, Ashley Montagu, tells us that acquired needs and unnecessary 'necessities' may well become drives as powerful as our most basic impulses, although they are quite unnecessary to our biological survival; on the contrary, they are a threat to it. We are using up the world's basic resources at a frightening rate, much of it in order to satisfy greed. We may want 100-page Sunday newspapers or two cars per family, but we do not need them. We may want a stereo or video but they should not come before food for the starving. But in our world, of course, they do. Indeed we can hardly see why they should not, as western economics is largely geared to satisfying unnecessary needs. When some members of a family are starving the parents do not feed the other children on caviar. In our larger family, society, this is precisely the sort of thing that happens. Nobody's fault of course; it's just the system.

It would seem reasonable for the West to settle for something less than it has been used to, if only for self-preservation, because eventually we will have left nothing for our own offspring, let alone others. The ruthless exploitation of nature by human beings, and one by another, has been held up to us almost as if it were a law of nature. But humans have not always and everywhere dominated and exploited nature, or each other. In many primitive communities the organic structure of society was egalitarian rather than hierarchical, as Murray Bookchin has pointed out.[2] The ideas of better or worse, superior or inferior, were alien to them. People and things were different, but no better or worse than other people or things. Difference and variety were prized rather than condemned. They had no idea of equality and freedom because they already had the actuality. The fact that such societies degenerated into hierarchical, unequal systems with social classes does not mean that they must always do so. The Hopi Indians, for instance, did all their basic jobs co-operatively, and the idea of competition was foreign to them. If co-operation is as much a part of natural law as competition, as Kropotkin has suggested, then perhaps there is yet hope for us all.

The idea that competition and conflict are dominant in human nature and basic to natural law ('Nature red in tooth and claw') has given support to the capitalist system. It makes use of such drives. But in his book *Mutual Aid*[3] Kropotkin presents us with another picture. Co-operation is seen to play an important part, and mutual aid is as much a part of nature as mutual conflict. He describes an incident quoted by Darwin in which a blind pelican was fed, and well-fed by other pelicans which brought fishes from a distance of thirty miles. Other observers have noted crows feeding a wounded crow, crows feeding blinded crows, a badger carrying away a wounded badger, and so on. One dreads to think what the world would be like if animals were to behave as viciously and ruthlessly as human beings. No animal has inflicted prolonged torture on its kind as human beings have. It is rare for animals to attack their own species; it is only too common for humans to do so. No animal aims to pollute the earth or the atmosphere, or threatens to blow the world up. They know instinctively not to destroy the earth which gives them life. Human beings in their rapacity and desire for self-advancement have smothered that instinct.

It is, then, not only our relationship with our fellow humans that is at stake, but our relationship with the planet as a whole. Neither *laissez-faire* capitalism nor communism can be the answer to the problem. We have to find another way. Happily the smothered instinct is not yet dead in everyone. More and more people are coming to realize that our present way of life is the way of death. Greed, facilitated by evermore sophisticated technology, is hastening us toward the abyss. Nevertheless all is not yet lost. There is still time to put on the brakes, and reconsider our position. There is still time, but not much time.

Notes
1. E.F. Schumacher, *Small is Beautiful,* Abacus, Sphere Books, 1974.
2. Murray Bookchin, *The Ecology of Freedom,* Palo Alto, California, Cheshire Books, 1982: 45.
3. Peter Kropotkin, *Mutual Aid,* Pelican, 1939: 62.

Competition and Co-operation • Work and Leisure

In war people work together for a common cause: the defence of their country. Miner and manager, soldier and sailor, poor and rich all pull together for the country's good. In peace the picture is rather different. Manager and miner are at each other's throats, the strong take advantage of the weak, the rich exploit the poor, the establishment batters the trade unions, the unions batter the public, individual is set against individual and class against class. The common cause is lost. All that seems to matter is one's own cause whether as individual, class or political party. This is called robust individualism by those it favours, and, by those who suffer from it, the ugly face of capitalism. Wars are won through co-operation, working together, helping each other. Peace is lost through competition, working against each other, doing each other down. Yet competition is elevated into a virtue, co-operation relegated to something to be tried only if everything else fails.

Co-operation between workers in the conflict of interests between management and workforce resulted in trade-unionism. Trade-unionism is essentially the substitution of collective for individual bargaining between employer and employee. Without it the individual had no chance against the employer. Trade-unions are the successors of the old craft-guilds, association of free craftspeople who banded together for their own welfare which were set up to protect themselves from abuses of power on the part of employers and authorities.

Capitalism introduced new factors into the relationship. It estranged employer from worker and it depressed wages as a consequence of over-production. The workers became little more than automata, dealing only with a single process instead of being responsible for the whole manufactured article. They became mere cogs in a machine, with wages the sole reason for work. The present-day troubles of trade-unionists are nothing new. Over a century ago legislation against trade-unions resulted in picketing and intimidation directed against both blacklegs and employers. This occurred so often that in 1875 Parliament brought in the

Conspiracy and Protection of Property Act. The present government's further legislation against the trade-unions is merely yet another step in the continuing alienation of employee from employer – pressure from employers, resistance by unions, legislation by government, further resistance by unions, and so it goes on.

The trade-unions were the progenitors of the Labour party and in general have always supported that party. They were considered to be to the left, to be radical, to be socialist. They wanted change. Nowadays the picture is different. They do not want change so much as more of the same. Many of their members now vote Conservative and the unions themselves have become rigid, conservative, and resistant to change. Even their values are no longer socialist. True, comradeship is still there, but as unions they seem to have adopted the ethics of their employers – money is everything, look after 'number one', me first and the devil take the hindmost. They seem to want to become not free partners in industry but merely more prosperous wage-slaves. In many cases of dispute it appears to be money rather than conditions of employment or co-operation with others that is now at issue.

The trade-union movement seems to have lost its way, and the middle classes have even succeeded in making trade-unionism a dirty word, yet the working classes would have been infinitely worse off without the unions, and so indeed would the whole country. One has only to look at those countries which have banned unions – totalitarians all.

We are now told that we are in a post-industrial age. Instead of more work we must think of more leisure. But we are as badly prepared for leisure as we were for work. Work implies making, leisure doing. Aristotle made a distinction between making (poiesis) and doing (praxis) a distinction which we often, perhaps too often, tend to overlook. Modern technology has enabled us to hand over the process of making to machines. Increased unemployment is a result, but we now have more free time to 'do' things on our own. The result, unfortunately, is aimlessness and idleness for we have been taught to associate doing with making, and there is not enough to make. The prospect is bleak as leisure-time increases and there is nothing to do. The astonishing efflorescence of Greek thought was largely the product of leisure. The Greeks were free to think and experiment because manual work was done by others. Nowadays the technology of basic subsistence presents us with a comparable situation. But we don't know what to do with our spare time.

Property

To Proudhon, property was theft. R.H. Tawney believed that theft became property. To Simone Weil private property was a vital need of the soul. But she restricted it to house ownership, a little piece of land round it, and the tools of one's trade. This sort of property, she considered, deprived no one while promoting independence and self-assurance.

One does not have to agree that property is theft to realize that something is very wrong with its distribution. But if property is theft it is not just theft from others, it is also theft from oneself, because a bit of oneself has gone into the property, and we are the less for it. 'Having', as Erich Fromm suggests, detracts from 'being'. The more we have, the less we are.

It is difficult to 'be' in a consumer society devoted to 'having' more and more of everything, where material growth is the aim and technological progress the means toward it. It is assumed, often without too much thought, that growth is healthy and essential. Indeed if we want to live in the sort of society which continually demands more and more then growth *is* essential. But do we have to go this way? Could we not perhaps, without shocking people too much, suggest that not only the government but our whole society has got it wrong?

Look where it has got us. It has brought us to a world in which millions are starving, where our growth has helped to bring about their deprivation, while the inhabitants of North America, amounting to about $7\frac{1}{2}$ per cent of the world's population, are using something in the region of half the world's basic resources. If this continues they will soon be using 90 per cent. This is growth; for $7\frac{1}{2}$ per cent of us.

But what about the millions in the third world scrabbling in the earth for what is left? How can people brought up to expect more and more ever put themselves in the position of those whose fate is increasingly to have less and less? A stark dichotomy lies not just between the western world and the third world, or between North and South, but also in the desperate condition of cities like Liverpool and, at bottom, in ourselves and our code of values. The more we have the less we are.

Recently our government appears to have been overcome by a mania for selling other people's property because it needed the money. One way of getting money is to squeeze nationalized industries and services, such as the railways. Unfortunately this pressure seems not to have saved or produced enough. A more profitable way is to sell off such services.

The telephone system, once the property of the public and paid for by them, has been sold off to private punters at a knock-down price, and since they have bought a monopoly they are very nicely situated. The gas industry was next in line. Having failed to get enough money from an additional tax on gas over and above the admitted needs of the industry, the next stage for the government was to sell it off. Another monopoly. Again a minority will make a nice little bit out of the sale of a public asset or public necessity. Water, too, an even greater necessity, will soon, we read, be at the mercy of the stock exchange. How long will it be, one wonders, before the idea occurs to someone in government to tax the air we breathe, or even try to sell it?

Money-Changers in the Temple

In his papal encyclical[1] of 1981 Pope John Paul said:

> We must first of all recall a principle that has always been taught by the Church, the *principle of the priority of labour over capital*. This principle directly concerns the process of production. In this process labour is always a primary *efficient cause* while capital, the whole collection of means of production, remains a mere *instrument* or instrumental cause.

He was not preaching Marx though one might be forgiven for thinking so; he was preaching Christianity. He was certainly not preaching capitalism.

That was some years ago and in the meantime the church seems to have found this teaching rather difficult to follow. There have been honourable exceptions of course, usually far removed from Rome, such as the liberal catholic bishops and priests in Nicaragua, El Salvador and the Philippines which his Holiness does not appear to have wholeheartedly welcomed.

As for the Vatican's own 'Banco Ambrosiano', it seems to have got its principles in a bit of a tangle, giving full priority to capital and a bit more. But then what is a bank for? In our civilization one cannot live without money and Christ's action against the money-changers in the temple would presumably today find little support among officials of the Banco Ambrosiano. So how do we relate this to the papal injunction in the encyclical? The principle of the priority of labour (people) over capital (money) seems to have been overlooked. This would not, of course, be remarkable in New York, Tokyo or the City of London but it seems a rather unfortunate omission on the Pope's own doorstep.

Note
1. 'Laborem Exercens'.

Satellite Countries

In Poland, once a proud and free country, now still proud but no longer free, the trade unions have been brought under control, the church muzzled, civil liberties curtailed, the police strengthened, and all aspects of life put under the strict control of the government. The direction of the country's foreign policy has, in effect, largely been handed over to a foreign power, the Soviet Union. Russia has installed military bases in Poland, in general to ensure that what Poland does agrees with what Russia wants.

In Britain, once a proud and free country, the trade unions have been brought under control, the church attacked, civil liberties curtailed and the police strengthened, while the government itself has become increasingly autocratic. Foreign policy appears to have been brought into line with, if not actually dictated by, a foreign power, the United States. America has installed military bases in Britain with many airfields, facilities and communications systems, to say nothing of nuclear weapons. Now, one reads, the US Air Force has declared an 'exclusion zone' in Britain. British pilots will no longer be allowed to operate in the air space bounded by Oxford and Banbury without permission from American air-traffic controllers. Moreover US military personnel are apparently not to be subject to British law. When the White House gives the orders Downing Street comes smartly to attention. Could not our prime minister and General Jaruselsky get together to decide how best to rid their countries of foreign domination? Or do they actually like it? The parallel is not, of course, an accurate one. We have not yet reached such a stage of autocracy in our own government, or of obeisance to another, nor does our restriction of liberties compare with Poland's, but we seem to be going that way.

Rulers and Ruled

Members of Parliament represent, or are supposed to represent their constituents at Westminster. They visit their constituencies, speak and hold 'surgeries', but how much do they really know of how most of us live? As MPs they are members of a cosy club with many privileges. Official cars whisk them from appointment to appointment, from House to home. Everything is laid on for them. While admitting that without such attention government would be more difficult, nevertheless it does appear to cocoon the subject of such attention from some of the asperities of the world outside.

To take an example, the Minister of Transport does not have to wait in the cold and wet for a bus that never comes. If he ever had to take a bus, he has no idea of what it is like now. No wonder, then, that public transport is in such a sorry condition. Improvement would no doubt soon be put in hand if the minister himself had to use it. The railways are run down and the subsidy cut to about half what the French and German governments are ready to pay for theirs. The prime minister, we are told, does not like railway travel. If one has a car and a chauffeur there is no problem. But roughly half the people of Britain have no car, and only a handful have a chauffeur. One way of widening the rift between Disraeli's 'two nations' is to cut public transport. Should we not be able to insist that ministers be forced to use public transport at least once a week?

To pursue the matter further, should not all politicians have to use the National Health Service rather than private health care? Should they not, at least for a period, know what it is like to live on Supplementary Benefit, to queue for this and that, to live, if only for a time, in the worst of our inner cities, to send their children to state schools? Impracticable you may say, but it would at least give them an idea of the sort of life their policies condemn others to, and no doubt would bring about rapid improvements in health care, social services, housing and education.

Waste

A consumer society such as ours produces an enormous amount of waste. Much of it is what is called bio-degradable and will eventually rot down, but equally much of it is not. For instance, plastics. Our rivers and seas are swimming with such waste, our beaches littered with it. The mania for packaging everything, even half a dozen nails, a single screw, three buttons or a tin-opener, often in a plastic pack of such indestructibility as to tax the strength of an all-in wrestler, may be all very well for the packaging industry, but it offers problems for the rest of us. More and more cars are good for the motor industry but they jam the roads, litter the pavements, and make life difficult for those who don't have them. Used car dumps in increasing number and size disfigure the countryside.

This sort of waste, however – the product largely of acquisitiveness and the fulfilment of unnecessary 'needs' – is a comparatively minor annoyance. At least, for the moment, it is not dangerous. But what, for instance, do we do about the disposal of nuclear waste? A nuclear reactor produces tons of waste which remains poisonous for thousands of years – plutonium for some 500,000 years. Where do we put it all, and how do we ensure that none of it escapes? We are still producing the stuff without having found satisfactory answers, and we propose to go on doing it increasingly regardless of public protest or of the threat to posterity. How can we make our ageing nuclear reactors safe for posterity – for the next few hundred years? Many are already reaching their age limit.

Even more disturbing is what to do with nuclear weapons. The world is stiff with thousands of them. Of course one day they may all be fired and that will presumably solve our difficulty and that of our children, grandchildren and great-grandchildren. But suppose they have not been fired and are still with us, menacing but so far quiescent, and they become obsolete, requiring to be replaced by other still more lethal weapons? What do we do with them all? And if we do succeed in 'rendering them safe', for how long? Ten years, 100 years, 1000 years, 20,000 years? Posterity will not thank us for leaving them such a legacy.

The attitude of governments to the increasing pollution of this planet as well as the secrecy with which any government envelops its own activities in this respect is deeply disturbing. There are leakages of nuclear waste into the Irish Sea. Who reports them? Not the nuclear authority if it can help it, not the government, but a small eccentric organization called Greenpeace. The French government stages a nuclear test explosion in the Pacific. Who monitors it? Greenpeace. The French government, furious at being thus monitored, blows up the Greenpeace boat and kills one of the crew. Japanese and Soviet factory-ships threaten the extinction of whales. Who tries to stop them? Again Greenpeace. I have a great respect for Greenpeace. In this violent, rapacious, destructive world of ours any organization trying to call 'halt' should be more than welcome. But Greenpeace is not welcome to the British, the French, the Japanese or Soviet governments who seem to be doing their best to pollute, destroy life and blow up those bits of the planet they can get their hands on. All with the best intentions, of course. But then governments never do anything without the best of intentions. It appears that they can't see further than the immediate benefit, or don't want to look. The future will have to take care of itself. The thought that they are mortgaging the future of our children for profit is of no consequence. The government is only in power for a few years at a time so it seems it has to do what it wants, when it wants.

In the past our dangers were mostly natural hazards; now they are predominantly of our own making. If we can make them, we can also get rid of them if enough of us want to, if we can persuade our governments to want to. There's the rub, for governments often appear to enshrine the worst instincts of any society they affect to represent.

Chernobyl

On 26 April 1986 the worst accident the world had ever seen occurred, at Chernobyl near Kiev in the Ukraine. The nuclear power station caught fire, part of the roof blew off, and a radioactive cloud was sent into the atmosphere. The first warning came from Sweden some 800 or 900 miles away, as the Russian government had admitted nothing. On 3 May the radiation cloud was detected over Britain. Two days earlier the concentration of radioactive iodine around Paris had reached ten times the permitted level, and the information was kept quiet. On 4 May, eight days after the Chernobyl disaster, there was a radioactive leak near Hamm in North Rhine-Westphalia. It was also concealed from the public, the authorities anticipating that the rise in radiation levels would be attributed to Chernobyl.

Since then there have been leaks at Hinckley Point, Somerset and Dounreay in Scotland. A further leak at Dungeness, Kent, sometime before had been kept quiet, while the leaks at Windscale-Sellafield continue year after year. The Sellafield leak of 1983 was found to be deliberate – highly radioactive material was knowingly pumped into the sea. It was concealed and only brought to light by a Greenpeace boat patrolling the area.

One can understand that politicians will never admit to error unless forced. One can see that since France now supplies some 60 per cent of its energy from nuclear fuel it is not exactly easy for the French authorities to admit to danger from radiation over the capital city. One can see that the Russian authorities, who are past masters at keeping not only their own people but the rest of the world in the dark, should not wish to broadcast the disaster. One can see that our own government, as advocates of nuclear development and its leader patently envious of French progress in this direction, should not wish to expose failures and dangers to public view. But there is a limit to personal susceptibilities, even those of politicians, for Chernobyl has shown us, if we did not know before, that we are all involved. The Chernobyl nuclear cloud expanded as far west as

Mid-West America and Alaska, as far east as Japan; indeed most of the northern hemisphere was involved, and this from just one site. There are eighteen nuclear plants in our country alone, and in spite of the American decision not to build any more after Three Mile Island the rest of the world has hundreds of them, and is still building more. The secrecy must stop and the public be given the facts, for without the facts no informed criticism is possible, and without informed criticism the danger is immeasurably increased.

Politicians are responsible to their own country. Now, however, they should be responsible to all countries. Nuclear disasters are not containable; nuclear radiation does not stop at frontiers. A nuclear disaster in France could affect much of the population of Britain, Belgium, Germany and Italy. We in Britain are facing a battery of nuclear plants, on the opposite Normandy coast while they face Dungeness. The Germans have built their first nuclear reprocessing plant at Wackersdorf in Bavaria, some 30 miles from the Czechoslovak border, and 75 miles from the Austrian frontier. The Austrian government called for its construction to be stopped. The Germans, nevertheless, continued with it. There seems to be a general tendency to site such plants close to frontiers with other countries.

Even closer to a frontier the French have built a huge reactor at Cattenom near Thionville, only 10 miles from both the Luxemburg and German borders. This reactor is scheduled to produce ten times the power of Chernobyl. If there were ever a Chernobyl-type disaster there the whole of western Europe would suffer and parts of the Rhineland, Alsace, Lorraine and the Saar probably made uninhabitable for generations. The Saar premier wrote to President Mitterand begging him to stop the project. The French government, like the Germans over Wackersdorf, ignored the plea and is continuing with the reactor.

There is, of course, a link between nuclear reactors and preparations for nuclear war, for weapons-grade plutonium can only be manufactured in such reactors. The link was, for a long time, officially denied because the authorities did not want such a link publicly known.

There is yet another danger. In a war there is nothing to stop a nuclear missile or even a conventional bomb hitting a nuclear reactor. Even if only one or two such reactors are hit the result, bearing in mind Chernobyl, would be devastating. No doubt all our nuclear reactors are scheduled as targets by the USSR. No doubt Russian nuclear reactors are similarly targeted by the West. It is claimed that if it comes to nuclear war it should, as far as possible, be contained. Targeting nuclear reactors, however, would make containment extremely difficult if not impossible.

110

The radiation from Chernobyl was apparently of the order of a 1-kiloton nuclear bomb explosion. NATO plans envisage that if the Warsaw pact were to launch a conventional attack and we were to respond with a first-use of nuclear weapons it would mean the detonation of 1000 kilotons over Germany, just as a start. The thought of Germany, or indeed western Europe, surviving a thousand Chernobyls is a sobering one when one Chernobyl can reach Alaska and Japan. But that would be only the beginning for one cannot doubt that the Russians would reply in kind.

The combination of immense destructive power in the hands of a handful of politicians apparently bent on witholding vital information from the people who elected them is a frightening prospect. What do we have? No longer a free society but all the makings of a militarist state. Not immediately perhaps but it is in the nature of governments to exercise power which they will tend to extend, whether openly or stealthily, unless held in check by a democratic electorate. But if the people are not informed, or are misinformed, such a check is no longer a valid one.

Slowly, gradually, under one pretext or another – defence of the realm, national security, best interests of the nation – freedoms will be whittled down, civil liberties curtailed, and the police forces strengthened not so much to combat crime as to control the public. In fact it is an acceleration of what is beginning to happen now. This is the beginning of a road, the end of which, unless we realize where we are going, is a form of totalitarianism under a powerful, centralized, technologically all-seeing, all-hearing, all-controlling state which Orwell's Winston Smith would recognize as not dissimilar to his own. Nuclear fission coupled with advanced technology, such as police computers and information banks, put immense power into the hands of a small group of politicians while emasculating the rest of us. I hope that this scenario for the future will never materialize but it is surely time we started considering it as a real possibility and using our democratic vote to ensure that democracy survives.

Nuclear Weapons

On 18 February 1961, a massive sit-down protest at the Ministry of Defence had been arranged by the Committee of 100, which was an activist off-shoot of CND. Audrey, myself and friends, who had joined the campaign shortly after its formation, took the tube from Hampstead to Trafalgar Square and sat with thousands of others as near as we could to the Ministry in Whitehall. Bertrand Russell, Michael Scott, and Russell's American secretary, Ralph Schoenman, were there. Russell stuck a notice of protest on the Ministry door. Russell, Scott and Schoenman with several others were arrested and sent to prison. From the point of view of publicity the sit-down was an enormous success.

The prevailing view of those in authority is that nuclear weapons ensure our security. I have to admit to some scepticism here. Nuclear weapons (with the exception of Hiroshima and Nagasaki) may not have been used, as yet, but there have been threats to use them, and numerous accidents and near-misses, almost never reported in the press which seems to be as secretive as *Pravda* in such matters. There were several occasions on which the Soviet Union threatened the use of nuclear weapons. It is known that in the Vietnam war President Nixon contemplated using nuclear weapons on more than one occasion but was persuaded against it. In addition there have been numerous 'incidents' and alerts. It does not look as if either side has been too deterred by the deterrent. According to Milton Leitenberg of Cornell University there have probably been some 100 specific deployments of nuclear weapons by the Americans during crises since the 1950s. No doubt there were similar deployments by the USSR, though the number is not known.

On 17 January 1966 a US Air Force B52 collided in the air with a K135 refuelling tanker. The B52 had four 25-megaton hydrogen bombs on board. The accident happened near Palomares in Spain. Two of the jettisoned bombs broke open spilling plutonium over a wide area. The US Air Force at first denied that nuclear weapons were involved. Then they sent in more than 1000 servicemen to clean up. They burned the crops, slaughtered the animals, told the inhabitants to burn their clothes and removed more than 1000 cubic yards of topsoil (plutonium apparently has a half-life of 25,000 years in soil). People in the immediate vicinity were sent to Madrid for health checks, but since plutonium can remain latent in the body for anything from 15 to 30 years no one can yet be sure who has not received a lethal dose. In Britain, American bombers fly daily from air-fields leased to the US Air Force. We are not told, and almost certainly will not be told, whether they are carrying nuclear weapons. Perhaps one day we shall know, by accident. We can only hope that the accident will not turn out to be a disaster.

Resistance to the abolition of nuclear weapons, or even a reduction of their numbers, is still strong, not only in the government but with many of the population. Perhaps the less we know the more we trust them, and we are not allowed to know very much. It is strange, however, how much anger and even hatred is stirred up in the hearts of normally well-behaved people when confronted with nuclear disarmers. The women of Greenham Common demonstrating against nuclear missiles have frequently been the butt of foul-mouthed louts and hooligans tearing down their wretched shelters, overturning their camp-fires, hurling excrement, urinating everywhere, smashing their car windows and generally causing as much damage as possible. Such incidents are rarely reported in the tabloid press which, in general, has no respect for the women but great respect for the missiles and those detailed to operate them. The courage and persistence of the women is phenomenal, the behaviour of their attackers totally degrading.

Confrontation

It is internal oppositions (in the same being) which make external
oppositions (between different beings) possible.

C.K. Ogden

Is not this the sad story of foreign politics? Why are the governments of
the Soviet Union and the United States so paranoid about each other's
intentions? Why does each power build up such a monstrous picture of its
opposite number? Can it be that they need each other as much as they
hate each other? Psychologically, does not each project its own faults and
designs onto the other? There are some things that a nation won't admit
to, or condemn, in itself but about which it is only too ready to castigate
another. This rather obvious fact should not need emphasizing were it
not that the governments on either side seem totally unaware of it.

The Vietnam war seems more acceptable if balanced by Afghanistan.
The rape of Hungary and Czechoslovakia is made to seem less heinous by
American aggression in Nicaragua, its support for the Greek colonels and
its destabilization of the democratically-elected government of Chile.
Each side can salve what's left of its conscience by pointing to the
misdeeds of the other. The rest of the world shakes in its shoes and hopes
the two 'super-powers' will not involve them too, for if they do come to
blows in their private quarrel the whole world will be the sufferer.

The American fear of encroaching communism must appear quite
inexplicable to the wretched peasantry of Central America. The Soviet
fear of capitalism can hardly be taken seriously by embattled villagers in
Afghanistan. Why are they made to bear the brunt of another's fears? The
Americans, of course, are feeding their fear by their own actions. Their
government's support for military juntas, for Somozas, Marcoses and
Pinochets against the poor and deprived is surely guaranteed to drive
people toward communism? The populations of Central and South
America are not communist at heart. They are largely Catholic but are
being relentlessly driven to accept communist aid because the United
States supports their oppressors. The way, surely, for the US government

114

to ensure that communism is no threat is to support the poor and oppressed rather than the rich? Similarly the way for the Soviet Union to ensure that capitalism is not a threat is again to support the poor and oppressed against the bureaucrats and *apparatchiks* who keep them poor and oppressed. The struggle is not so much between East and West as between 'haves' and 'have-nots'. With unerring pig-headedness both the United States and the Soviet Union have chosen to support the 'haves'. In Ethiopia the Soviets, while largely ignoring the starving, have supplied massive military aid to the government. The Russians have given propaganda fodder to the capitalists, the Americans to the communists. Each has got the other to do its own work for it.

But why do we all have to take sides in this dangerous confrontation? The two super-powers have split the whole world, with a few courageous exceptions, into two opposing camps. Does each side have to arm itself with enough nuclear weapons to kill everyone on the planet ten times over in order to maintain such a confrontation?

Terrorism

One man's terrorist is another man's freedom fighter – a truism too often ignored. To the Arabs the Israelis are terrorists, and their own men freedom fighters. To the Israelis the Arabs are terrorists, and so it goes on. If beauty lies in the eye of the beholder, so does terrorism. Pascal summed it up:

> 'Why do you kill me?'
> 'Well, don't you live on the other side of the water? If you lived on this side, my friend, I should be a murderer, and it would be wrong to kill you like this. But since you live on the other side, I am a brave man and it is right.'

And yet terrorist and freedom fighter are not really the same under different names. What distinguishes one from the other? A freedom fighter who kills or threatens to kill innocent, unarmed people in his attempt to free his country is a terrorist. If he confines his threats and actions to the armed forces and government of his country's oppressors he's no terrorist. Fighting between fighters is not terrorism, but threats, abduction and the killing or wounding of civilians or unarmed people most certainly is. The problem is, often, how to separate the innocent from the involved, the unarmed from the armed and, consequently, freedom fighting often degenerates into terrorism. Consider as examples the Kurds, the Basques, the Irish and the Palestinians. Terrorism is a cancer arising out of resentment, frustration and a feeling of injustice. People who do not so suffer rarely breed terrorists.

Terrorism however often fosters terrorism in those who hate terrorism. An attack on terrorism can well become a terrorist attack. Take the case of the American response to the belief that Gadaffi was behind terrorist attacks affecting American citizens. The US fleet and air force attacked Libyan towns and bombed and killed many of Libya's citizens including children. A nation of 220 million had 'taught a lesson' to a nation of three and a half million. Goliath had beaten David into the ground. The Americans felt proud. Now, at last, after the defeat of

Vietnam they could hold their heads high and 'walk tall' again; they were strong again. They had shown the world they meant business, and were amazed and hurt when much of the rest of the world, including some of their own NATO allies, did not appear to agree with them wholeheartedly. Weren't the Americans destroying terrorism? Why should the US have to go on taking whatever that 'mad dog' Gadaffi chose to inflict on them?

But the rest of the world, though loathing Gadaffi and his terrorist activities, also loathes other terrorist activities not supported by Gadaffi, and this attack was one of them. Moreover, it transpired that Gadaffi was almost certainly not responsible for the terrorist attacks which provoked the American bombing of Libya.

It occurred also to non-Americans that the United States had supported terrorist activities in other parts of the world for decades – in Chile, in El Salvador, in Nicaragua, for example. It was behind the invasion of Cuba and the attempted assassination of Castro. It had given its blessing to the Greek colonels with their regime of oppression and torture. It had backed, if not actively at least tacitly, the ruthless regimes of Somoza, Baptista and Papa Doc. During the Vietnam war the American use of 'agent orange' has, it is now reported, resulted in some babies being born without eyes and some without brains.

Terrorism, brutality, torture and bloodshed are not confined to Libya, Syria, Iran, South Africa, or the Soviet Union. The western world is guilty also. The attack on Libya was an instance of one form of state terrorism attacking another. Britain has little of which to be proud, either. Its prime minister, without fully consulting the government or even considering the people, had agreed that America's Libyan adventurism could use this country as a springboard, or stationary air-craft carrier, for whatever punitive action it might pursue.

It appears that, in some respects at least, the future described in George Orwell's *Nineteen Eighty Four* is beginning to materialize. Great Britain on that occasion did indeed become 'airstrip one'. 'Newspeak', 'doublethink' and the 'mutability of the past' are taking over. The slogan 'war is peace' is now followed by 'our terrorism is freedom fighting', your 'freedom fighting is terrorism', and perhaps most frightening of all 'ignorance is strength'.

117

Approach to War

In 1936 I was living in Paris, teaching English and doing some work for a rather eccentric little paper of minimal circulation called *Nouvelles de l'Inde*. It was run by a French Quaker from her apartment in the Boulevard Montparnasse. She had been married twice, once to a classical scholar and then to a parliamentary Député, but was now widowed. She knew many people in the literary world and was a sister-in-law of the writer, Romain Rolland. She was also a pacifist and supporter of the Rassemblement pour la Paix, two of its protagonists being Rolland and the well-known author of *Le Feu,* Henri Barbusse. Madame was a great admirer, indeed a friend, of Gandhi who stayed with her on one of the rare occasions when he visited Paris. I was shown, with due reverence, the actual bed in which the Mahatma had slept. Her brother-in-law had written a biography of Gandhi, while the paper she edited was largely devoted to reporting and supporting Gandhi's aims in India.

The main living-room of Madame's apartment had a grand piano but little other furniture except books. Piles of books littered the floor while others were heaped on such chairs as there were and covered the top of the piano. On occasion, her son, who I believe had some position in the Agence Havas (the French equivalent of Reuters), would come in, remove the litter of papers from the top of the piano, play some Bach and depart. He never seemed to stay for long, and I never got to know him.

As a disciple of Gandhi Madame believed in *ahimsa* – no injury to any living thing. This made life difficult, for unfortunately the apartment attracted mice as if they knew that no death sentence would be pronounced on them. With the odd practicality which occasionally afflicts idealists, Madame got a long cage made, capable of incarcerating four or five mice. When she had enticed them in she would canter down the stairs, out into the Boulevard, run to the Place de l'Observatoire and set them free, not far from the restaurant 'La Closerie des Lilas'. I'm sure they must have fared better at the Closerie, which had a reputation for its cuisine, while being at greater danger to life. Madame was a kind-hearted soul and her solicitude for mice was paralleled by her hospitality for human beings, two of whom, a young Russian student and an Indian gentleman, occupied beds in her apartment but were never seen during the day.

As perhaps one might have guessed Madame was a vegetarian. Whenever she went out she took tins of cous-cous and other vegetarian food with her, often strapped to her person. Indoors, as befits a child of nature, she went bare-foot, but she nevertheless had her stockings at the ready, pinned to her undergarments so that they dangled down beside her legs, available for donning at any moment. From her elaborate belt, dangled steel-rimmed spectacles, bunches of keys and various small receptacles, the contents of which I never discovered. Madame, I regret, is no more. I have pleasant memories of her and of the opportunity afforded me to get a little French literature into my head as I oscillated between her library and the Bibliothèque Ste. Genéviève. Such a character is a sad loss in a grey world of conformity.

As a result, no doubt, of my sojourn in Paris and with the influence of *Nouvelles de l'Inde* and Romain Rolland's *Au Dessus de la Mêlée* I developed a marked antipathy to war and war-mongering. However, when a few years later war actually broke out and Germany invaded Poland, France, Belgium, Holland and was threatening Britain herself I capitulated. Perhaps I should have stuck to my ideas, as many did, and become a conscientious objector, but either my conviction was not that firm or the force of circumstances was too much for me. In the spring of 1940 I became a soldier in the Devon Regiment. Later, as I had some knowledge of French, German and Italian, I was transferred to the Intelligence Corps and was sent, in the best British Army tradition, to a country where none of those languages was spoken: Sierra Leone. Its capital, Freetown, was at that time the largest convoy port in West Africa on the route round the Cape. The Germans, having overrun France and taken over the neighbouring French colony of Guinea, had installed a U-boat base there which threatened any convoy destined for Freetown harbour.

It was assumed that there would be talk in the port's bars and markets of interest to the enemy. It was therefore decided that I should become a temporary civilian and report on any leakage of information. Since such an assignment could not be carried out by someone wearing khaki drill, I was kitted out with civilian clothes, even to the extent of evening wear with white jacket and black cummerbund. I was then settled into the City Hotel (readers of Graham Greene's *Heart of the Matter* will recognize the scene) and provided with a 'cover' job. I became a laboratory assistant at the Liverpool School of Tropical Medicine's establishment just outside the town, under its chief, Professor Blacklock who was necessarily privy to the deception.

I knew nothing of tropical medicine but was soon introduced to the mysteries of using a microscope and a microtome. Whether anyone was actually taken in by this rather farcical masquerade I have no idea. The loose talk in Freetown's bars and bazaars was of such evident banality that trying to make serious reports on it took some ingenuity. I cannot remember one case that merited more than a cursory investigation. Eventually my CO decided that I might be used more fruitfully elsewhere and I became a soldier again.

After a year and a half in West Africa I was sent back to England. I had missed most of the bombing and found my unit HQ comfortably installed in Oriel College, Oxford. From there I went on a German intelligence course at Cambridge where again I was comfortably put up in St John's College. The course was, as far as I was concerned, brought to an abrupt close by the invasion of Italy. I was shipped out to Sicily, landing in the middle of a bombing raid at Augusta. For the next two and a half years I saw more of Italy than I have ever seen of Britain. I was attached to one unit after another – to a base sub-area, to the 1st Airborne Division, to Eighth Army Headquarters, and so on, finally ending up in Austria.

The war had not cured me of my anti-war leanings. Although I myself had been lucky I knew of many others who hadn't. One friend was killed in the bombing raid as we were disembarking at Augusta. At Anzio and Cassino the slaughter was horrendous. One could not help but ask why. How did it all happen? To what end? The answers were far from satisfying. They remain so.

Now that nuclear weapons are stacked in their threatening thousands on both sides, to be loosed perhaps by those who have never known war at first hand, some other answer will have to be found. As matches are kept out of the reach of young children, so nuclear weapons should be kept out of the reach of irresponsible adults. Unfortunately irresponsible adults now have matches that could set fire to the whole world.

After the War

Shortly after the war my wife Audrey and I were both working in the East End of London – in East India Dock Road. All around were bomb-sites, acres of waste-land, broken homes and broken lives bequeathed by Hitler's bombers. The East End had suffered to an extent hardly imaginable by the West End. On the bomb-sites were hundreds of shacks and rickety, patched-up caravans. The people may have been bombed out of their homes but they were not quitting. On the Isle of Dogs by the West India Docks a woman and two children were living in an apology for a tent. There was no sanitation. Buckets of excrement, euphemistically called night soil by officials, were simply emptied into man-holes and drain-grilles in the street. The City, with St Pauls, the big banks and finance houses, was only 3 or 4 miles away. Travelling westwards one could not help but be aware of the contrast. We were two nations then. We are two nations now, if not more. The land fit for heroes to live in seems hardly nearer now than it did in Lloyd George's day. The desolation of the bomb-sites is replaced by the desolation of Brixton and Toxteth. We are supposed to be a rich nation. It does not make sense.

Some years ago Audrey and I had an eccentric holiday touring the industrial cities of the north-west – the Potteries, Stoke, Liverpool, Manchester, Wigan and, on another occasion, Glasgow. My wife's interest was housing conditions, a subject in which she had become something of an expert. What we saw in Liverpool was, if anything, even worse than in London's East End with which we were only too familiar, having worked there for thirteen years. In Liverpool we saw whole families living in one room, beds jammed against each other, mattresses soaked in urine, clothes-lines loaded with underwear strung from wall to wall, cooking done over an open fire, and above all the unmistakeable smell of poverty. This was years before the Toxteth riots, but at the time we wondered why people were not rebelling then. However, poverty appears to weaken resistance more often than it inflames revolt. Similar conditions are now being repeated in the sordid bed and breakfast hotels which the government seems to prefer to building new and badly needed housing.

In Glasgow we toured the Gorbals. Audrey had been asked to investigate the idea of housing homeless families in an old ocean liner moored in the Clyde, so we went for advice to Strathclyde university. The idea was, of course, impracticable for a variety of reasons. The homeless, then as now, were under great pressure from the social services who were set up to serve them. After three months even mothers and children were separated, children and even small babies being taken 'into care'. It was not until 1964 that accommodation for whole families began to be provided. We came back from our tour depressed and enraged that such conditions should exist in one of the world's most prosperous countries.

War and Torture

During the 1960s the Peace Research Group of Des Moines, USA, did some research on militarism. Over 2,000 people in North America were interviewed individually on a scale of attitudes. Further studies over the years up to 1976 produced the following picture. Those scoring high on militarism tended to be extrovert, misanthropic, neurotic, subject to greater discipline in childhood, socially irresponsible, egotistic, and conformist in their personal relations. They were also likely to be dogmatic, intolerant, rigid, nationalist, patriotic, racist, punitive, conservative, against social welfare and for *laissez-faire* capitalism.

It was suggested that an over-disciplined childhood led to misanthropy which in turn led to authoritarianism, which led to conservatism and nationalism, which led to militarism. Bearing in mind that the Research Group probably found what it wanted, there seems to be more than an iota of truth here. One can certainly think of one or two politicians whom this picture appears to fit.

During the present century militarism has had a field day. Never before has so much been spent on the art of mass killing. While Britain's exports of manufactured goods have reached a new low, her exports of weapons of war are thriving. We are one of the major exporters of arms in the world. Indeed, in the top four, the others being the United States, the Soviet Union and France. Together we export arms to some 100 nations, many of them in the Middle East.

Military expenditure is staggering. In 1985, world spending hit around the 850 billion dollar mark, which is about 200 dollars for every human being on earth. 100 million dollars an hour went into the art of killing people. It is not thought of as killing people, of course. It is called security, or defence, and known to be good business. Not even the government likes to use nasty words. Britain, indeed, was fastidious enough to change what used to be known as the War Office into something a little less direct. It is now known as the Ministry of Defence. Weapons may be used, of course, for display or to deter, but they are also for use as weapons. Since

1945 the world has seen 120 wars, an average of three a year, while since the beginning of the century some 3,500 people a day have been killed in war. This may be good for the military-industrial complex but for little else. The tragic absurdity of it all beggars description.

As for torture, the prospect looks equally grim. The torture of one person by another is, or ought to be, a shameful act. Torture by an institution is, if anything, worse. We have all heard of Torquemada and the Spanish Inquisition, but we probably say to ourselves that that was 500 years ago and we do things differently now. Unfortunately we are still doing it. The practice has spread, moreover, to governments. Some seventy nations throughout the world employ torture as an instrument of policy. And who, you may ask, would permit the manufacture and export of instruments of torture? It appears that some governments do not blench at it, including our own. There are some trades, surely, where even market forces should not be allowed a free rein?

The Purpose of Science

We are told we live in a scientific age, but there are many kinds of scientists and some of them may be said to hold the world at their mercy. Mostly these are neither top-notchers nor unpretentious technicians. They are the reliable, competent, middle-of-the-roaders who produce what is required of them and rarely appear to question what they are doing. They work for large multi-national chemical trusts, armament firms, the nuclear weapons industry, the KGB, the CIA, military juntas and repressive regimes of all political colours as well as for the armed forces of democratic governments. Morality does not enter into their reckoning. If something can be done and they are required to do it – a new poisonous gas, an improved nuclear war-head, sophisticated methods of controlling populations by force – they get on with it, no questions asked. Science is neutral, they say, and manage to turn a blind eye to its application, which may be anything but neutral.

In the past it was often the church that was obscurantist. Nowadays obscurantism often characterizes some aspects of science. Alfred North Whitehead tells us that the obscurantists of any period are largely the practitioners of the dominant methodology, and that since today scientific methods are dominant it is the scientists who are obscurantists. Many scientists appear to do their best to prove Whitehead right, while condemning such assertions as perverse and heretical.

What then is science for? Is it for the good of mankind, or is it for itself? The general feeling among scientists appears to be in favour of the latter. There should be no constraints on science. Everything is permissible. It is its own reason for existence; anything else is sentimental. Now, after experiments on prisoners in German concentration camps, after Hiroshima and Nagasaki, and after such experiments as grafting a monkey's head onto another live monkey and claiming success when the animal managed to live for a brief moment, people are beginning to question the all-permissibility of science.

In ancient Greece, Hippocrates recognized the dangers of unethical medical practice and instituted the Hippocratic Oath, not only for the protection of patients but to safeguard the honour of medical practice itself. More recently, Einstein was one of the first to question the all-permissibility of science over the use of nuclear fission. Now, and not before time, a growing number of scientists is beginning to concede that there might be a moral aspect to what they are doing. It is rather late in the day, and the opposition is strong, but at least it is a start.

Technology[1]

We live in an increasingly technological society. But what is technology? Basically it is an extension of our sensory-motor involvement with our world. It extends our sense of sight by means of binoculars, telescopes and microscopes, television sets and videos; our sense of hearing by stethoscopes, listening devices, telephones, bugging devices, radio transmitters and receivers; our sense of touch through delicate instruments capable of detecting the least movement or changes of heat and cold; our sense of smell through smoke and gas detectors; our muscle by means of lifts, hoists, cranes, wrenches, spanners, can-openers, bottle-openers, bicycles, cars, trains, ships, planes and so on.

As well as our sensory-motor equipment, technology also serves the rational processes of the mind. It increases enormously the speed of calculation through computers and pocket calculators, as well as thought itself. It does not invent or create, for invention and creation are non-rational, though it can be programmed to do almost anything of a systematic, logical, rational nature.

If humans are machines, then technology makes us giants, extending our capabilities to the stars on the one hand, to sub-atomic particles on the other. The whole material world is the playground of technology. If the material world were the only world, progress in technology would seem to bring about the millennium. But there are other worlds. Technology has nothing to say to us in the world of values, of justice, of art and its appreciation, of fellow feeling, or indeed of all those matters which slip through the mesh of 'Maya', the world of appearances, and which make life not only bearable but meaningful. Technology adds nothing to such non-material worlds. Indeed it subtracts from them. The speed and strength together with the sophistication of advanced technology seduce us from value and judgement, from feeling and appreciation, and present us with the Golden Calf of speed, size and strength for our worship.

As technology grows it becomes more complicated and mostly more expensive. The can-opener can be bought and operated by a child, the bull-dozer by a company, but the super-sonic bomber and the moon-rocket can only be ordered by governments. Technology means the concentration of more and more power into fewer and fewer hands. The danger of this must surely be obvious, but it is nevertheless rarely heeded. It threatens such democracy as we have and edges us inexorably towards rule by a tiny minority over which we will have no real control. War does much the same thing, concentrating power in the hands of a few while at the same time weakening the voice of the people. War, fortunately, does not continue for ever and democracy has a chance to re-assert itself. But what about technology?

Technology was originally developed to make life easier, to lift people out of a life of poverty and drudgery, but the benign servant has grown into a ruthless master. In the nineteenth century industry was welcomed as being in the service of people, but the ideal soon turned in effect into people in the service of industry. In the twentieth century the same thing is happening with technology. Rather than technology in the service of people we are now seeing that process reversed. Weapons of mass destruction threaten us as never before while we ourselves are reduced to little more than nameless nonentities, numbers to be juggled with in an economic statistic. Gandhi once remarked that any machine which helped an individual had a use, but for those machines which concentrated power in a few hands, turning people into machine-minders, there should be no place at all.

The danger with advanced, sophisticated technology is made worse by the type of society which has developed it, and by which, in turn, society is inevitably shaped. It is not a technology for the deprived many but for the privileged few, for those who already have more than enough. A society which will spend hundreds of millions of pounds on military technology or on getting people onto the moon, rather than spend it on hospitals, public-transport systems and schools, or on basic agricultural implements and tools for those who desperately need them, is not a balanced society, nor is it a just one. It would appear that if we are to regain control of our technology rather than bow the knee to it, our social system will need to be radically changed from an authoritative, hierarchical society to a more democratic, egalitarian one; for the type of technology determines the type of society. They feed on each other.

Technology could prove of immense benefit to countries of the third world.[2] A simple technology geared to the individual, to the small farmer, to the medium-sized commune or the co-operative could be of inestimable value. But third-world governments are not, it seems, all that interested in third-world people. They are, in general, autocratic and tend to be too easily seduced by the values of capitalist and communist governments of the more developed nations which they attempt to emulate. They willingly buy what is offered, such as sophisticated technology when the real needs of their people are simple and basic. The bureaucrats of the third world pay vast sums which they can ill-afford for technology which the people as a whole cannot use. Enormous technological schemes are put in hand requiring complicated and expensive machinery.

The needs of those in power are met by what the developed nations have persuaded them to buy: military weapons, television sets, refrigerators, Mercedes cars, computers, and so on. The needs of the mass of the people are not met. Cash crops are produced for sale to the western world while their own people starve. This fact, which surely must be glaringly evident, tends to be overlooked because the West can no longer think in basic terms. It can only think in terms of its own economics to benefit the privileged few.

In primitive societies social production was designed so that it fitted in with environmental needs. People recognized that they could not kill off the herds of beasts on which they depended, nor tear down forests. They needed to maintain their food supply, to keep the earth in good shape, not only for themselves but for posterity. They lived in partnership with their environment, giving back to it as much as they got out.

Technology has put an end to this balance of nature. It has exchanged understanding and mutual benefit for power and dominance. It has enabled man to rape and pillage the earth, to exhaust the supplies of fossil fuels, to change the vegetation, the drainage and even the climate of whole areas. Ruthlessness, greed and speed, coupled with technology, have started us on a path which, if persisted in, may well leave posterity with little to live on and could well, indeed, forbid life itself.

With Pandora's box now open, how do we control what has escaped? A change of attitude and a change of direction are what are surely needed. A change of values, and a change of system. *Laissez-faire* capitalism is no answer, nor is totalitarianism. Both are power giants which can only think in terms of power and domination which create aggression and conflict. If the earth is to be saved from further spoliation, and us with it, we must begin to start thinking, not from the top down, but from the bottom up. Decentralization and free association, small groups and co-operatives should be replacing centralized power and direction. It has been tried before, of course, in the Ukraine in 1918 until overrun by the

Bolsheviks, and in Catalonia in the 1930s until brought to an end by General Franco and the civil war. Both attempts were brought to a sad end, the one by the left, the other by the right. Others have been set up since as more and more people come to realize that basic necessities must come before unnecessary luxuries, and that the only way to bring this about is by taking the initiative into our own hands, not through government. The farmer's plough must take precedence over the city speculator's car, organic manure over chemical fertilizer. Instead of pillaging the earth for fossil fuels for energy, we need to look to basics – sun, wind and water – solar energy, wind power, and water power. Three of the original 'elements': fire, air and water! The fourth element, earth, we have already half exhausted, and the planet is still young.

Notes
1. The best book I have read on the subject is by Jacques Ellul, *La Technique ou l'Enjeu du Siècle,* Armand Colin, 1954, Eng. trans, *The Technological Society,* Cape, 1965.
2. David Dickson, *Alternative Technology,* Fontana/Collins, 1974.

Rhythms of Life

Everything dances to its own peculiar measure. Halley's comet was apparently first observed by the Chinese in 466 BC and has come round again every seventy-six years with clock-work regularity. It was recorded as an observation in the Bayeux tapestry. It first appeared this century in 1909–10, and round it came again in 1986. The earth circles the sun in 365.24 days year after year. The moon circles the earth in roughly 28 days, month after month, while the surface of the sun also rotates in 28 days. The period of menstruation is again 28 days or one lunar month; the period of gestation ten lunar months. The rhythm of the human heart is, on average, some seventy-two beats a minutes. The rhythm of respiration is normally some sixteen breaths a minute. There are rhythms of brain activity, of cell development, of nerve sensibility, of adrenalin production, as well as many other bodily rhythms.

The body is like an orchestra – a counterpoint of interlocking rhythms, harmonious in health, discordant in disease. Rhythms of heart, of breathing, of digestion, of sleeping and waking co-operate in an harmonious whole. One group of cells controls and modifies the rhythms of another in mutual tuning and adjustment. This inner counterpoint is matched by the rhythms present in the outer environment.

There are the obvious rhythms of light and dark, of summer and winter, of the ebb and flow of the tides. The harmony of our internal rhythms helps to prevent the disruption by outer rhythms, assimilating such of those rhythms as sustain life, and indeed make life possible. Nature as a whole dances to a stately rhythm, the dance of Shiva, to hundreds of intertwined, interacting, overlapping rhythms, a dance in which we wittingly or unwittingly participate.

Harmony – External and Internal

Boethius, the fifth-century philosopher, divided music into three types: *musica mundana,* the harmony of the spheres, *musica humana,* the harmony of the human soul and body, and *musica instrumentalis,* the actual playing and singing of music. In *musica mundana* and *humana* we see the influence of Pythagoras, and such musical proportions seemed to penetrate everywhere in medieval Europe. The great gothic cathedrals, for instance, were conceived as 'music in stone'; the musical proportions found in them were not there by chance but by deliberate design. The scholars of Chartres, well-schooled in Plato's *Timaeus,* not only found musical proportions in Solomon's Temple but built them into their own cathedral. Many buildings in fifteenth- and sixteenth-century Italy incorporated the proportions of music and Pythagorean ratios. Andrea Palladio was one architect so influenced, which his 'Palladian' buildings demonstrate so admirably.

Modern architecture has yet to incorporate such proportions. Le Corbusier, it appears, made use of the Divine Proportion or Golden Section in his book *Le Modulor,* but without success in concrete. Though I'm inclined to think the fault lies with the architect rather than with the proportion which did quite well for the Parthenon.

External harmony is reflected internally. 'Musica mentis medicina maestas' – 'music is the medicine of a melancholy mind'. From Orpheus onward music has been credited with magic properties. In the eighteenth century a Dr Mitchell wrote a dissertation: 'On the art of healing in the presence of ancient music and with the help of songs.' The Pythagorean physician Alcmaeon emphasized the importance of 'harmonia' in the interaction of the various parts of the body with the whole, and of the whole body with its environment. Others have claimed that music contributed to the health of both mind and body, assisting in the circulation of the blood and 'dissipating vapours'.

More recently, experiments have been made on the effect of music on the health and growth of plants. Apparently they respond in a remarkable way to certain kinds of music, leaning towards the origin of the sound, as well as benefiting in growth and health. The music they seem to prefer is Bach, Haydn, Beethoven, Brahms and Schubert, and the most appreciated of all is Ravi Shankar playing classical Indian music. They also respond to jazz, but not to rock-music. In Soviet Russia it is reported that patients have been treated successfuly with music, and have benefited by listening to the recorded sound of the sea. The threads of music and rhythm run through everything: uniting in harmony, fracturing in discord. Perhaps we should pay a little more attention to music than we do.

Utopias

What lessons do Utopias hold for us in the approaching twenty-first century? If the question were put in a Gallup poll the answers would probably add up to 'Not much'. And yet, down the centuries, from Plato's *Republic* onwards writers have been tempted to sketch out one ideal state after another. Isaiah Berlin in an essay on Giambattista Vico lists also Thomas More, Patrizzi, Doni, Campanella, Francis Bacon, Harrington, Winstanley, Foigny, Fénelon, Swift and Defoe, counting only those in the Renaissance and early seventeenth century.[1] In the late seventeenth and eighteenth centuries there were many more. In addition we have Fourier's *Phalansteries,* Robert Owen's experiment in Lanark, and William Morris' *News from Nowhere* and *A Dream of John Ball.* Finally we can list H.G. Wells, George Orwell and Aldous Huxley, and that is by no means all

Utopias may be seen as ideals, or as terrible warnings such as Orwell's *Nineteen Eighty Four.* Plato's *Republic* can be seen as a Utopia to be copied or as a dreadful warning to be avoided. Simone Weil considered that the different categories of citizen in the *Republic* stand for different parts of the soul. She claims that Plato expressly states this: 'Perhaps there is a model of it in heaven for whoever wishes to see it and, seeing it, to found the city of his own self.' One never knows at quite what level of meaning to take Plato, but since he was fond of allegory it seems likely that the allegorical comparison with mind or soul is probably the right one.

Some of the Utopias, for example Plato's and Thomas More's, feature a form of communism, and William Morris', socialism. Within the last few years there has been a crop of such books which, though perhaps not strictly Utopias, nevertheless adumbrate ideal states in which people are seen in co-operation rather than in conflict with nature and the environment. Among them are Pedler's *The Quest for Gaia,* Schumacher's *Small is Beautiful,* Barbara Ward's *Progress for a Small Planet,* Marilyn Ferguson's *Aquarian Conspiracy* and books by Leopold Kohr, Gordon Rattray Taylor and Fritjof Capra. It is in these, rather than in the Utopias of the past, that ideas for the future lie.

Note

1. Isaiah Berlin, essay, 'Vico and the Ideal of the Enlightenment', in *Against the Current,* OUP, 1981: 121.

Man's Inhumanity to Man – Woman's Humanity

Ever since the Industrial Revolution, and especially since the rise of technology, we appear to have been on a sort of collision course between people, and between people and the environment. Before that time, the lack of technology meant that our inhumanity to others was limited and our effect on the environment minimal. Now the story is rather different. We can destroy the environment for ever and blow everyone off the face of the earth at the touch of a button or the failure of a fail-safe mechanism. We and the earth we live off have never been in so much danger. This should be a sobering thought, but it does not appear to have sunk into our rulers. Unfortunately with so much lethal power at our disposal we are no wiser than we were before.

The major curses we face today are not so much nuclear weapons, war, poverty and starvation in themselves, but the attitudes of mind which bring them about – selfishness, greed, fear and lust for power. Moreover, these are predominantly male faults. Females are inclined to be less obsessed with power, and tend to be less greedy and selfish. They also tend to be less destructive. If we want a more balanced, less greedy, less power-hungry world then we must see that women are given their full value, not simply as mothers and wives, but as equal arbiters of our destinies. A difficulty seems to be that women have for so long become accustomed to limiting their influence to the home and family, largely to please men, that most are ill-equipped for wider views. This need not be prohibitive since it is surely obvious that most men are also as ill-equipped in their own way. But men do not think they are, while women do. If women were to think themselves as competent as men, without losing their feminine values, then we might begin to see a change in our fortunes.

Somehow or other the predominance of male values must be ended, and a balance created with an increased appreciation of female values. It is difficult to see men bringing this about; but women could. They have the intelligence, and their subtlety is often more than a match for the male's

135

greater strength. But without confidence they will not do it. In our male-dominated world self-confidence more readily finds a home in confrontation than in co-operation. Co-operation requires greater courage for it implies the willingness to drop one's defences in a common cause. Fear of co-operation is a disease affecting our world leaders. But co-operation is now becoming a necessity. And co-operation comes more naturally to women.

How should women set about this re-orientation of values. In 412 BC Aristophanes suggested a solution to the persistent warmongering of men in his play *Lysistrata*. The women, led by Lysistrata, not only refused to co-operate with their menfolk but withheld their favours and foreswore their beds until the fighting stopped. I am not suggesting that Aristophanes has the answer to the present state of barely-controlled belligerence, let alone the problems of poverty and starvation; that would be too easy.

In autocratic states, military regimes and dictatorships, women have little power. In democracies, however, women have immense potential power if they care to use it. In Britain, for instance, more than half the population is female. Women have, in the ballot box, the possibility of swinging the nation over to a better balance of female–male values, of curbing male domination, of putting thoughts of peace before those of war. They have the capability, and the possibility. If anyone doubts it let them read the anthropologist Ashley Montagu's *The Natural Superiority of Women*. The capability is there, but is there the will? Some men have seen the writing on the wall and are working for change, but if change is to come about and a proper balance restored it will surely largely be due to the efforts of women.

It is a tall order. Can those obsessed with money and power be won over? It seems hardly likely. They will surely go on as before, for as long as they can. It would appear that only a nuclear war, or a succession of Chernobyls might persuade them to change their minds.

On this small globe circling the sun a tragi-comedy is playing itself out – a comedy perhaps for some, a tragedy certainly for others – but which may soon become a tragedy for all. Our humanity is neglected while we play with fire. Hundreds of thousands starve while a few spend countless millions shooting rockets into outer space. Millions are killed by the weapons we sell to others. All over the earth people are imprisoned, tortured, deprived of their freedoms, executed or blown up in the name of some national, religious, racial, economic or political doctrine. Exacerbating this mess seems to be the readiness of governments, including our own, to sell improved technology and armaments to the thugs, the juntas, the regimes who perpetrate such horrors. The Russians, the Americans, the French, and ourselves all mouth words of peace while feeding the dogs of war. To say 'It has ever been so' is a complacent platitude. It is getting worse and our means of making it worse increase from year to year.

The need for a change of heart and a change of mind could scarcely be more pressing. But the darkness of the night foreshadows the dawn. The pendulum reaches the bottom of its sweep and begins to rise and in the reciprocal balance of opposites, Yang begins to yield to Yin. In the words of *Ecclesiastes:* 'to everything there is a season'. Perhaps, now, the time is ripe. 'Give me a place to stand and I will move the earth,' said Archimedes. Do we not see a glimmer of a fulcrum in the massive participation of women in CND, at Greenham Common, in 'Green' parties and associations everywhere, and in their demand to be given some choice as to how their children should be born, housed, fed, schooled and educated?

End Piece

Our world is fragmented but below the surface there is unity, coherence and meaning. Wholeness, or holism, is there for the finding, and now we are beginning to find it. We have spoken of the curious way in which like reaches like across barriers of space and time, and of the way in which parallel inventions and ideas come to the surface in different people at the same time, each unaware of the other's involvement (e.g. Newton and Leibniz and the invention of the calculus.) Perhaps the fact that holism, or wholism, now seems to be catching on all over the world is an instance of this sort of subterranean, or superterranean communication. Could this, perhaps, be related to the concept of 'morphogenetic fields'? Such a concept goes far beyond Kepler's *'facultas formatrix'*, or formative faculty. It suggests that hidden morphic or morphogenetic fields give regular shape and movement not only to the material universe but also to the mind, determining not only growth and form, but the shape and direction of thought itself.

Such formative fields may be seen as distant relations of Plato's 'forms' or 'ideas' but Dr Sheldrake believes that similar forms resonate in harmony and reinforce each other across space and time. The morphic field, apparently, not only guides the growth of seed and flower and caters for that other biologist, C.H. Waddington's 'chreodes', or formative paths but, in bringing in the idea of morphic resonance, broadens the concept of pattern-formation immeasurably. Reaching far beyond Darwin and Lamarck it could, perhaps, help to explain why Fabre's wasp was able unerringly to paralyze and deposit its eggs in a beetle so that it could provide food for the growing egg.

The biologist Rupert Sheldrake and the physicist David Bohm have come together in agreeing that morphogenetic fields can be seen as relating to Bohm's ideas on 'wholeness and the implicate order'. It looks as if here we have a tie-up with the hologram and with the hidden pattern and order implicit in the cosmos. What emerges is an astonishing picture – a holographic universe in which fields of resonance and

138

patterns of development combine, in which unity and diversity come together, in which each part is distinct, yet each part contains all. If this picture is anything like true then we have, surely, a meaningful cosmos in which we play a minor, but nevertheless important part. Not all of such links or associations have been proved, in as far as they can be proved at all, but the general picture is beginning to look a little more acceptable.

A fragmented world? If we have fragmented it perhaps we can now see that beneath the surface there is unity, order and wholeness, and perhaps this may give us the heart to attempt to put what is fragmented together again. We will never completely succeed, but the exercise of trying might well help to prevent the whole vast fabric of our material world disintegrating at our touch. It is not necessary to do everything at once. Perfection in any case is unattainable. Just a small shift in the right direction would do for a start. Scheler, like Bergson, considered the universe a device for the making of gods. Perhaps more modestly we might look on it as a device for the development of women and men and, conversely, as a device for the further development of the cosmos through the agency of men and women. We are all in it together.

Bibliography

Adams, George, *Physical and Ethereal Spaces,* London, Rudolf Steiner Press, 1965.

Allport, Gordon, *The Nature of Prejudice,* New York, Anchor Books, 1958.

Allsop, Kenneth, (ed.) *The Environmental Handbook,* Pan Books, 1971.

Ashley Montagu, M.F., *Darwin, Competition and Co-operation,* 1953; *The Natural Superiority of Women,* 1953; *The Direction of Human Development,* London, C.A. Watts, 1957; *Man and Aggression,* OUP, 1973.

Barfield, Owen, *Saving the Appearances,* Faber, 1957.

Barzun, Jacques, *Science, The Glorious Entertainment,* London, Secker & Warburg, 1964.

Bateson, Gregory, *Mind and Nature,* Fontana, 1985.

Berger, John, *Ways of Seeing,* BBC and Penguin, 1972.

Beveridge, W.I.B., *The Art of Scientific Investigation,* Heinemann, 1950.

Blair, Lawrence, *Rhythms of Vision,* Paladin, 1976.

Bleibtreu, John, *The Parable of the Beast,* Paladin, 1970.

Boethius, *Consolations of Philosophy,* Penguin Classics.

Bohm, David, *Wholeness and the Implicate Order,* Routledge, 1980.

Bookchin, Murray, *The Ecology of Freedom,* Palo Alto. California, Cheshire Books, 1982.

Buber, Martin, *I and Thou,* New York, Scribners, 1958.

Burnet, John, *Early Greek Philosophy,* A & C Black, 1930.

Capra, Fritjof, *The Tao of Physics,* Fontana, 1978; *The Turning Point,* Fontana, 1983.

Cassirer, Ernst, *Language and Myth,* New York, Dover, 1953; *An Essay on Man,* New York, Doubleday, 1956; *The Philosophy of Symbolic Forms,* New Haven, Conn., Yale, 3 vols, 1953–7.

Clardy, J.V., *The Philosophical Ideas of Alexander Radischev,* Vision, 1964.

Critchlow, Keith, *Order in Space,* Thames & Hudson, 1969; *Time Stands Still,* London, Gordon Fraser, 1979.

Cornford, F.M., *Plato's Cosmology: The Timaeus of Plato,* Routledge, 1956.

Darlington, C.D., *Genetics and Man,* Pelican, 1966.

Dickson, David, *Alternative Technology,* Fontana, 1977.

Eliade, Mircea, *The Myth of the Eternal Return,* Routledge, 1955; *The Two and the One,* Harvill Press, 1965; *Myth and Reality,* Allen & Unwin.

Ellul, Jacques, *The Technological Society*, Cape, 1965.

Emme, A., *The Clock of Living Nature*, Peace Publishers, Moscow, 1953.

Benjamin Farrington, *Greek Science*, Pelican, 1953.

Ferguson, Marilyn, *The Aquarian Conspiracy*, Granada, 1982.

Findlay, J.N., *The Discipline of the Cave*, Allen & Unwin, 1966; *The Transcendence of the Cave*, Allen & Unwin, 1967.

Franz, Marie-Louise, von, *Number and Time*, Rider, 1974.

K. Freeman, *The Pre-Socratic Philosophers*, Oxford, Blackwell, 1949.

Fromm, Erich, *The Fear of Freedom*, Routledge, 1961; *To Have and to Be*, Abacus, 1979; *Beyond the Chains of Illusion*, Abacus, 1980; *Man for Himself*, Abacus, 1947, *The Sane Society*, Routledge, 1956.

Fuller, Buckminster, *Utopia or Oblivion*, Pelican, 1972; *The Buckminster Fuller Reader*.

Galbraith, J.K., *The Affluent Society*, Pelican, 1962.

Gardener, Martin, *The Ambidextrous Universe*, Penguin, 1967.

Ghyka, Matila, *Geometrical Composition and Design*, London, Tiranti, 1956.

Guthrie, W.K.C., *A History of Greek Philosophy*, CUP.

Happold, F.C., *Mysticism*, Pelican, 1971.

Heisenberg, Werner, *Physics and Philosophy*, Allen & Unwin, 1963.

Holbrook, Bruce, *The Stone Monkey. An Alternative Chinese Scientific Reality*, New York, Wm. Morrow, 1981.

Huntley, H.E. *The Divine Proportion*, New York, Dover, 1970.

Huxley, Aldous, *Ends and Means*, Chatto, 1938; *The Perennial Philosophy*, Chatto & Windus, 1947.

Illich, Ivan, *De-Schooling Society*, Calder & Boyars, 1971; *Celebration of Awareness*, Calder & Boyars, 1971; *Medical Nemesis*, Calder & Boyars, 1974.

James, William, *The Varieties of Religious Experience*, Fontana, 1968.

Jones, Roger, *Physics as Metaphor*, Abacus, 1983.

Jordan, Martin, *New Shapes of Reality: Aspects of A.N. Whitehead's Philosophy*, Allen & Unwin, 1968.

Kirk, G.S. & Raven, J.E., *The Pre-Socratic Philosophers*, OUP, 1937.

Kitto, H.D.F., *The Greeks*, Pelican, 1965.

Kohr, Leopold, *The Breakdown of Nations; The Overdeveloped Nations*.

Kropotkin, Peter, *Mutual Aid*, Pelican, 1939.

Kumar, Satish, *The Schumacher Lectures*, Abacus, 1982.

Langer, Susanne, *Philosophy in a New Key*, New York, Mentor Books, 1951.

Lean, Geoffrey, *Rich World Poor World*, Allen & Unwin, 1978.

Livingstone, R.W., (ed.), *The Legacy of Greece*, OUP, 1924.

Merleau-Ponty, Maurice, *The Structure of Behaviour*, Methuen, 1965; *The Phenomenology of Perception*, Routledge, 1962.

Murchie, Guy, *Music of the Spheres*, Secker & Warburg, 1961.

Nicoll, Maurice, *Living Time*, London, Vincent Stuart, 1952.

Nouy, Lecomte du, *Human Destiny*, Mentor Books, 1963.

Pedler, Kit, *The Quest for Gaia*, Granada, 1979.

Plato, *The Timaeus,* Penguin Classics, 1965.

Polanyi, Michael, *Science, Faith and Society,* OUP, 1946; *Personal Knowledge,* Routledge, 1958; *The Tacit Dimension,* Routledge.

Popper, Sir Karl, *Conjectures and Refutations,* London, 1962.

Prigogine & Stengel, *Order out of Chaos,* Fontana, 1985.

Ribot, T., *Essay on the Creative Imagination,* Kegan Paul, 1906.

Rousseau, Jean Jacques, *The Social Contract* and *A Dissertation on the Origin of Inequality,* J.M. Dent, 1916.

Russell, Bertrand, *Mysticism and Logic,* Unwin Books, 1963.

Sambursky, S, *The Physical World of the Greeks,* Routledge, 1963.

Sarton, George, *Ancient Science through the Golden Age of Greece,* Harvard University Press, 1959.

Scheinfeld, Amram, *Women and Men,* Chatto & Windus, 1947.

Scheler, Max, *The Nature of Sympathy,* Routledge, 1954.

Schneer, C.J., *The Search for Order,* English Universities Press, 1960.

Schroedinger, Erwin, *What is Life? Mind and Matter,* CUP, 1967.

Schumacher, E.F., *Small is Beautiful,* Abacus, 1974; *A Guide for the Perplexed,* Abacus, 1978; *Good Work,* Abacus.

Schwarz, Walter and Dorothy, *Breaking Through,* Green Books, 1987.

Sheldrake, Rupert, *A New Science of Life,* Paladin, Granada, 1983.

Stace, W.T., *A Critical History of Greek Philosophy,* Macmillan, 1920 (last ed. 1967).

Talbot, Michael, *Mysticism and the New Physics,* Routledge, 1981.

Taylor, A.E., *Plato, The Man and his Work,* University Paperbacks, 1966.

Taylor, Gordon Rattray, *The Doomsday Book,* Thames & Hudson, 1970; *Rethink,* Pelican Books, 1974.

Tawney, R.H., *The Aquisitive Society,* G. Bell & Sons, 1952; *The Radical Tradition,* Pelican, 1966; *Religion and the Rise of Capitalism,* Penguin, 1938.

Thompson, D'Arcy, *On Growth and Form,* abridged edn, CUP, 1963.

Thompson, E.P. *et al., Protest and Survive,* Penguin, 1980.

Toynbee, Arnold *et al., Man's Concern with Death,* Hodder, 1968.

Upanishads, The, Penguin Classics, 1970.

Valens, E.G., *The Number of Things,* Methuen.

Valéry, Paul, *Regards sur le Monde Actuel,* Paris, Gallimard, 1945.

Waddington, C.H., *Towards a Theoretical Biology,* Edinburgh University Press, 1970; *Tools for Thought,* Paladin, 1977.

Ward, Barbara, *Progress for a Small Planet,* Pelican 1979; *Only One Earth,* (with Rene Dubos), 1972.

Watts, Alan, *Nature, Man and Woman,* Abacus, 1976.

Whitehead, Alfred North, *Science in the Modern World,* CUP, 1926; *Adventures of Ideas,* CUP, 1933; *Nature and Life,* CUP, 1933.

Whyte, Lancelot Law, *Accent on Form,* Routledge, 1955; *Aspects of Form,* Lund Humphries, 1968.

Wilson, F.A., *Crystal and Cosmos,* London, Coventure, 1977.

Woodhouse, Tom *et al.*, *People and Planet,* Green Books, 1987.
Worsley, Peter, *The Three Worlds,* Weidenfeld & Nicolson, 1984
Young, Arthur M., *The Geometry of Meaning,* San Francisco, Delacorte Press; *The Reflexive Universe,* San Francisco, Delacorte Press, both 1976.

Name Index